Dakota

Dakota

An Autobiography of a Cowman

W. H. Hamilton

With an Introduction by
Thomas D. Isern and Foreword
by Virginia Hamilton Baldwin

South Dakota State Historical Society Press
Pierre, South Dakota

Library of Congress Cataloging-in-Publication Data

    Hamilton, William Henry, 1863-1945.
        Dakota : an autobiography of a cowman / by W.H. Hamilton ; with an introduction by Thomas D. Isern ; and foreword by Virginia Hamilton Baldwin.
          p.   cm.
        Includes bibliographical references (p.   ) and index.
        ISBN 0-9622621-5-3 (pbk.)
        1. Hamilton, William Henry, 1863-1945. 2. Pioneers—South Dakota—Butte County—Biography. 3. Ranchers—South Dakota—Harding County—Biography. 4. Butte County (S.D.)—Biography. 5. Harding County (S.D.)—Biography. 6. Frontier and pioneer life—South Dakota—Butte County. 7. Ranch life—South Dakota—Harding County.
        I. Title.
    F657.B9H36   1998   98-46844
    978.3'403'092—dc21   CIP
      [b]   rev.

Picture credits: All illustrations are property of the South Dakota State Historical Society, State Archives Collection, except for those on the following pages: pp. 83 (top), 86 (bottom), from Virginia Hamilton Baldwin, Norfolk, Conn., John William Hamilton, Hephzibah, Ga., Joel Alan Hamilton, DeMarest, N.J., and Sarah Constance Hamilton, Kennesaw, Ga.

Manufactured in the United States of America

01 02 03 04 05 06 07 08 09   9 8 7 6 5 4 3 2

Contents

List of Illustrations

Foreword to the Reprint Edition

by Virginia Hamilton Baldwin

When my sister Sarah Hamilton and I spent a week attending an Elderhostel program in South Dakota, we were struck by the rugged beauty of the land, so different from our eastern hills and wooded valleys. The Badlands especially fascinated us, and as we drove around visiting various tourist sites, we saw many books on the history and development of the Dakota Territory. It reminded us that our grandfather, William Henry Hamilton, had written about his own experiences in Dakota as a young cowman. Where we were driving so easily in our car was where he had ridden horses and driven cattle many years ago.

His manuscript, "Dakota: An Autobiography of a Cowman," had been published in 1938 by the South Dakota State Historical Society. After our return, I called Nancy Tystad Koupal at the society to inquire if the story could be republished as a book, and she felt that it would be a worthwhile project because there is presently much interest in how the West was developed.

Our family also felt that it would be a fitting memorial to William, who was a very unusual man. The original manuscript was written many years after the events described therein, in the form of letters to his son Harold Henry Hamilton, who felt that such a life should not go unrecorded. Will, as his wife always called him, had a prodigious memory and could recall the names and dates connected with the most minor of incidents. He also loved to tell stories and had the ability to convey his enthusiasm and delight through the written word. Harold typed up these letters as a continuous story, and the State Historical Society printed it in Volume XIX (1938) of the *South Dakota Historical Collections* series, along with another long work of historical interest.

William loved South Dakota, as is clear from his story, and he expected that he would live there always, with his family and friends nearby. As his children grew, however, he and his wife Nancy Ellen realized that the lack of schools in the territory was a real problem. They both believed that a good education was extremely important, and finally, even though it meant giving up a life they loved, they moved away from beautiful Dakota to Fulton, Missouri, where a good high school and good colleges were located.

Their children fulfilled expectations. William Jackson, the oldest, went on from Westminster College in Fulton to gain a Ph.D. in History and to become a professor at the University of Missouri Teacher's College in Cape Girardeau, Missouri. Sarah Lucretia graduated from Synodical College in Fulton, married, and spent the rest of her life caring for her invalid mother and her husband William Walthall. She was a lovely, kind, and dedicated woman. Ray Showalter graduated from Westminster and then went on to graduate from the Massachusetts Institute of Technology, becoming an engineer. He had a successful career with Union Carbide and was honored by his home town of Fulton for his achievements. Harold Henry, who was born after the family's move to Missouri, went from Westminster College to Harvard Medical School and became a highly honored physician and surgeon in Plymouth, Massachusetts. Fulton also called him back home to pay him honor.

Nancy Ellen (who lived to the age of 99) and William lived on the farm in Fulton until his death at age 80 of cancer. He rose at five A.M. to milk the cows and to do all the other hard work of farming without ever a complaint, but it was clear that he missed the West. He kept many books on the West and particularly western adventure paperbacks in tall stacks all over his house. Every week until his death, he received through the mails a copy of the *Belle Fourche Bee*. He loved horses and never used a tractor. He often took us grandchildren in the big old black buggy to swim and fish in a nearby river, where he taught us to clean and fry up the fish over a campfire. Riding the ponies he kept for us and buggy rides to town for ice cream were fascinating entertainments for children who knew only automobiles and suburban life. William believed that automobiles would be the ruin of America, and he may have been right. In 1940, Ray took his father to South Dakota for a nostalgic visit, which I am quite sure was the only time William went back to see the places he loved so much.

The writing of the letters that form this book must have given him a great deal of pleasure. Though written long after the experiences and events in time, his enjoyment of the life he describes with such clarity gives the story a sense of immediacy, rather than being a nostalgic memoir.

Nancy Ellen and Will's life on the Great Plains can hardly be imagined now. The hardships, dangers and privations, the wild weather, the great distances did not stop them. They brought his parents, brothers and sister, cousins, and friends to see how free and wonderful it was and to live there also. The beautiful open land and the kindness, honesty, energy, and good humor of the people Will describes make it easy to see why Dakota had such a hold on their hearts.

Will Hamilton's grandchildren, Virginia Hamilton Baldwin, John William Hamilton, Joel Alan Hamilton, and Sarah Constance Hamilton, feel fortunate to have Will's story and are delighted at the chance to have it told again. We wish to dedicate this new edition to the memory of our brother:

Samuel Robert Hamilton
13 May 1926-22 May 1996.

Introduction to the Reprint Edition
Ways and Habits
of the West

by Thomas D. Isern

Well into his autobiography, William Henry Hamilton recounts a conversation with his brother Jone. By this time the brothers are veteran homesteaders of the Belle Fourche River Valley and pioneering ranchers of the Cave Hills. Jone has been back east to visit kin and friends in West Virginia, and the visit has been a disappointment. People back there are not the same anymore, he says. William (W. H. in formal correspondence, Will to immediate family, Virginia Bill to his friends in South Dakota) reflects on this comment and realizes that his brother has it all wrong. "We were the ones who had done the changing," the writer concludes. "We had fallen into the ways and habits of the West, while they were going on in their same old way back in the Blue Ridges" (p. 89).[1]

This statement was not an admission of guilt on his part; it was an expression of satisfaction. W. H. Hamilton wanted nothing in life so much as to absorb the ways and habits of the West. In an unpublished Foreword to his autobiography, he outlines with pride his family history of pioneering. His great-grandfather, Robert Hamilton, was a Scottish immigrant and a Revolutionary War veteran who pushed across the Alleghenies to settle in western Pennsylvania. He and his wife, Sarah Brooks Hamilton, raised eleven children there, the oldest of whom was James, grandfather of W. H. Hamilton. Coming home a veteran of the War of 1812, James Hamilton decided "the old home country was getting too settled up" and so relocated to western Virginia (later Preston County, West Virginia), where he and his wife raised their eleven children. The next-to-youngest of these was W. H.'s father, Aaron Jackson Hamilton, who married Lucretia Dennison. They would raise three children, of which W. H. was the eldest. Coming home from service in the Union Army during the Civil War, Aaron Hamilton took over the family farm.[2]

As a boy growing up in those West Virginia hills, W. H. Hamilton thrilled to stories of the frontier days. Although he emulated his male ancestors, he listened raptly to the stories passed on not only by grandfather James but also by his elderly aunt Sarah Baker. "Nothing did me quite so much good," he wrote "as to get Aunt Sarah started telling me of her childhood, and [the] way they lived when she was young, how they raised nearly everything they lived on, [the] way they made their clothes, and planted and gathered their crops."[3]

These family narratives foreshadowed much of what W. H. Hamilton would write about in his autobiography. His grandfather had hunted for subsistence and kept two large dogs for bear-hunting because bears were a menace to the family's hogs. Later, the younger Hamilton would hunt big game and birds for the ranch table, complain of the depredations of wolves on cattle in South Dakota, and bring in hunting dogs to eradicate them. The men in the family back east kept and prized fine horses, used mainly for handling timber. Much of the following western autobiography is devoted to the handling of horses. W. H. Hamilton knew nothing but strong women in his lineage and appreciated them. His mother, he writes, "had both large and small spinning wheels," and the women carded, spun, and wove their own linen and wool.[4] Later he describes his own wife, brought west to the ranch in the Cave Hills, as a good rider and a ready housekeeper who killed a wolf in the ranch yard with a revolver (pp. 140-41).

Hamilton treasured his family traditions in the West Virginia hills and enjoyed life there. He and other young swains attended the three-day meetings of the Dunkards, which concluded with a feast and the ceremony of the washing of feet. The men rode to the meetings horseback with their sweethearts swinging up on a blanket behind. Hamilton at this time was courting his future wife, Nancy Ellen Showalter. The young man was nevertheless discontent. The hill folk had only small farms and worked them in simple fashion. "Our fields were not more than ten or twelve acres in size," he writes, and "one man could not take care of more than six or eight acres of corn" that was hand-planted, cross-plowed, and hand-hoed. Hay was cut with a scythe and raked by hand. Few farmers even owned a wagon, let alone a mowing machine, horse rake, cultivator, or reaper.[5]

Hamilton got little schooling, but what he did get awakened dreams far more grandiose than the picayune farming of his home district. "There was only one branch of learning at our school that I really liked," he recalls, "and that was history. . . . I was always anxious to get books to read which told of pioneer life and early settlement of the different parts of the United States, such as those dealing with the lives of Daniel Boone, Kit Carson, David Crockett, and hunters like John Zane Wetzel, and others." Then there was the story of his own restless grandfather, who as an old widower followed the example of the aged Daniel Boone and went west one more time to homestead in Missouri. "I was always interested in the Western country," Hamilton confessed, remembering: "When I read about the goldstrike in the Black Hills in '76, I decided I was going to see that country if I ever grew to manhood, although I said nothing to anyone of my decision. . . . I had my heart set on a frontier country."[6] Adding further incentive to moving West was Uncle William B. Hamilton and his family who moved first to Missouri, then homesteaded in Sully County, Dakota, before moving to Butte County in 1883.[7]

When a couple from Iowa, originally from West Virginia, came back home to West Virginia in 1883 and mentioned that they needed a hired hand, W. H. Hamilton, then twenty years old, persuaded his parents to let him go back with them. "I did not tell any of them that Iowa was only a temporary stopping place," he writes. He was on his way to the Dakota Territory.[8] As it turned out, his parents had similar ambitions and would also be heading west soon, bringing Hamilton's sister Rose and brother Oliver (called by the nickname "Jone"). It is at this point that the published autobiography takes up the story.

Hamilton's *Dakota* is the story of a homesteader, a rancher, a family man, a hunter, a farmer, a community builder. The events he recounts took place in what is now Butte and Harding counties in the northwest corner of South Dakota, which until statehood in 1889 was Dakota Territory. After leaving West Virginia in 1884, Hamilton worked briefly in Iowa and Nebraska, then traveled by rail and coach to a frontier setting more to his liking—the ranch run by his Uncle William B. Hamilton, known as Missouri Bill, on the Belle Fourche River, just north of the Black Hills of Dakota. In 1885, young W. H. Hamilton, soon to be known as Virginia Bill, bought a relinquishment, paying a homesteader to let him take over his claim. His parents arrived and took a claim also. Meanwhile, as homesteaders began farming the valley, large herds of cattle and their owners continued to arrive from Texas, as they had since the late 1870s, to establish great open-range ranching operations throughout the area.

During the late 1880s, both the affairs of the developing community and those of Hamilton's own life, as he recounts, took important turns. The deadly winter of 1886-1887 killed cattle by the tens of thousands and drove most of the big outfits out of business. The tragedy was not unmitigated, however, for the demise of the great ranches left the range open for smaller operators. The new aspiring ranchers were encouraged by the arrival of the Fremont, Elkhorn & Missouri Valley Railway and the founding of the town of Belle Fourche as a cattle shipping point in 1890.[9] Hamilton's father Aaron, known as A. J., thereupon scouted range some seventy miles north, along the face of a great butte called the Cave Hills, and the Hamilton family put together a modest herd, which they drove north to the headquarters they had chosen on Jones Creek.

Over the next few years, Virginia Bill divided his time between his homestead on the Belle Fourche and this ranch (a partnership with his father and brother) in the Cave Hills, although the tone of his narrative makes it clear his heart was out on the cattle range. There, he participated in the vigorous community life of Cave Hills ranchers who got together for roundups, branding bees, and, most important, fall cattle drives to the shipping points of Belle Fourche and Dickinson, North Dakota. The ranch had a rival for his affections, however, as he was carrying on a courtship by mail with his sweetheart in West Virginia, schoolteacher Nancy Ellen Showalter. He had visited back home in late 1887 and early 1888 (thereby missing the most deadly winter in the history of South Dakota). In early 1893, he went back, married his schoolteacher, and brought her to the Cave Hills ranch. A son, William Jackson Hamilton, was born in 1894; a daughter, Sarah Lucretia Hamilton, in 1896; and a second son, Ray Showalter Hamilton, in 1898. A third son, Harold Henry Hamilton, would come in 1903 after the family had left South Dakota.

The ranch was graced with additions and improvements also. In 1896, Hamilton built a wood-frame ranch house for his growing family, and that fall, he and the neighbors joined together to buy five hundred fine Hereford bulls in Chicago. Nevertheless, the father of three was now considering giving up the ranch because he worried that his children would grow up without society or advantages. In 1897, he sent his wife and children back east while he scouted for a more settled place to relocate. He eventually moved the family to another farm on the north side of the Belle Fourche River, where he spent a few years raising corn and wheat, keeping a small cowherd, and breeding hefty Poland China hogs. Finally in 1901, he elected to leave South Dakota entirely, buying a farm near Fulton, Missouri, and moving his family there. During the 1930s, the aged Will Hamilton, having raised his children in the more settled circumstances of central Missouri, thought more and more about his frontier days, which led to the writing of *Dakota* thirty years after the events it describes.

Hamilton viewed his experiences with affection, but without rosy lenses. Hardship figures prominently in the narrative, and climate and weather were the basis for much of it. Beginning with a harrowing journey by coach and sleigh to get from the railroad in Sidney, Nebraska, to Deadwood (pp. 2-9), Hamilton suffered a series of dangerous encounters with blizzards and cold. Young and brash, the West Virginian seemed slow to learn that, although most winters north of the Black Hills were open, temperatures could plunge for a few days to dangerous lows of thirty to forty below. After he rode from the ranch over to Ashcroft for his mail on a forty-below day, the postmaster at Ashcroft, fearing for the man's life, refused to allow him to ride home (pp. 78-79). Despite the generally open winters, during which cattle could graze on buffalo grass cured on the ground, the Hamiltons put up plenty of hay for feeding when there was snow cover. Heavy snow also presented the danger of snowblindness. What the ranchers hoped for, of course, was the chinook, that warm, dry wind descending the east face of the Rocky Mountains, melting away snow, and providing respite from the long winter.[10]

Some of Hamilton's initial recollections of Cave Hills ranching had to do not with cold but with heat—prairie fire. On first arrival at the ranch, he rode out northwest to help his new neighbors fight a fire on Bull Creek, building backfires and beating them out ahead of the blaze. Then on the way home, spotting another fire to the southwest, he rode off to help fight it (pp. 52-53). Later he recounts how, on a quiet day, they put out a fire by splitting a dead steer with an ax and dragging it over the flames (pp. 107-8).

Whereas fire fed on drought, the dreaded gumbo became pernicious with every rain. Modern soil surveys of Butte and Harding counties show that the soils of the Belle Fourche River Valley are heavy loams, and those of the Cave Hills area are somewhat lighter loams. In between— the route frequently traversed by Hamilton—lies a belt of clayey prairie with difficult soils, particularly those of the Linler-Lismas and Pierre-Kyle associations, the popular name for which is "gumbo."[11] Pioneering South Dakota historian Doane Robinson observed, "Gumbo when slightly wet is very adhesive and roads and paths are practically impassable when it is in that condition."[12] Writers of the WPA guide to South Dakota referred to this gumbo belt, forty miles wide, as "a desolate region looking like a sea with long rollers that have suddenly become petrified," possessing "a black soil of almost unbelievable viscosity when wet." Brigadier General George Crook, who campaigned through the area, found it to be a horse-killer.[13] Settlers such as Hamilton complained of the gumbo, but they also learned to arrange their lives around it, simply conceding they could not travel after a rain. The image of hard-riding cowboys immobilized by difficult soils certainly detracts from the romance of the open range, but it was a reality of their everyday lives that Hamilton could not fail to note (pp. 99-100).

As was that bane of life on the northern plains, the mosquito. It may be impossible for people of the northern plains to explain to people from other parts of the country the extreme discomforts caused by the mosquito menace, but Hamilton comes close (pp. 38-39, 106-7). Most of his mosquito complaints come when he is traveling on the prairies, which makes sense. Those gumbo soils are not too permeable. Even in a country with only thirteen inches average annual rainfall, water would pool up after any rain and furnish ample breeding opportunities for the insects.

No larger fauna seriously imperiled settlers of the area, but some were nuisances and others caused economic loss. Hamilton mentions rattlesnakes and narrow escapes (p. 23) but refers to the reptiles more as interesting natural features than as problems. An early naturalist in the area averred, "One may drive or ride a couple hundred miles without seeing one," although Hamilton might not have agreed (p. 105). Porcupines were a hazard only to dogs who had not yet learned to avoid them. Wolves, however, menaced cattle. Hamilton is indefinite as to the extent of losses, but undoubtedly they occurred. The same naturalist confirmed the "gray or buffalo wolf" to be still "quite plentiful" in 1914 and predicted the beast "will probably continue to give some trouble to horse and cattle raisers for some years to come."[14]

Despite his exasperation with wolves, Hamilton and his brother Jone clearly had great times hunting them. He recounts that they used trailing hounds to flush the beasts into the open and greyhounds to run them down and kill them. They also raised crossbred dogs that would both trail and kill. In January 1896, the *Belle Fourche Times* reported that Hamilton "says their pack of trail hounds is making life a burden for the wolves in the Cave Hills country. Last year they crossed the trail and the greyhounds, and they now have dogs who can run as fast on a trail as by sight. The only trouble is, the wolves are getting so scarce that the boys are losing lots of fun. He thinks they have solved the wolf question."[15] With such hunting pressure and because of their susceptibility to strychnine poisoning, wolves were in fact virtually extirpated from the area by the 1920s, and the Northern Great Plains subspecies that bedeviled Hamilton, *Canis lupus nubilus*, became extinct soon after.[16]

Hamilton's generation of settlers had little experience with American Indians. When he mentions them, he speaks of them more as a hazard of nature, a peril passing with the frontier, than as people. A local historian later would relate, "The last Indian scare in Harding County was in 1890, shortly after Sitting Bull was shot by the Indian Police on the Standing Rock Reservation. Some of Sitting Bull's band started up the Grand River toward Harding County." Some settlers fled to towns in the Black Hills, "while others remained in groups, fortifying themselves," but, in the end, "no Indians were seen."[17] Hamilton describes a similar experience (pp. 61-63).

Even though there were hazards in this environment, it also provided sustenance and pleasure to Hamilton and his contemporaries. When he was homesteading on the Belle Fourche in the 1880s, he and others made frequent expeditions north into plains-and-butte country to hunt pronghorn, usually called antelope. Plentiful in Hamilton's time, these animals were nearly wiped out by 1910 as a result of the efforts of such subsistence and market hunters as Hamilton and his family, who sold the carcasses in Black Hills settlements, but fortunately pronghorn are numerous again since the 1950s. White-tailed jackrabbits and native grouse also provided food and income. Both sharp-tailed grouse and sage hens were abundant, but the sage hens were easier to kill. The young ones—preferable for eating because they did not taste so strongly of sage—were so easy to approach they were dubbed "Fool Hens."[18]

Once he had moved to the ranch in the Cave Hills, Hamilton's favored game was mule deer or, as they were called then, black-tailed deer. They were more common in this province of the plains than were white-tailed deer; Hamilton considered it a great oddity when he shot a whitetail (pp. 147-48). Zealous hunters would nearly eliminate both species on the plains by the turn of the century, but both have rebounded to abundance since the 1950s. Hamilton also records several encounters with bighorn sheep, which earlier settlers claimed could be found on every butte. This subspecies, *Ovis canadensis auduboni*, rapidly declined to extinction, but the area has since been recolonized by a modest population of another subspecies.[19]

Not only game but also the wild fruits of the region graced the Hamilton table. His accounts accord with the common experience of settlers throughout the Great Plains. Gathering berries and fruits was a family social activity and the special province of women, with men joining in. The Hamiltons and friends harvested and used the same wild plants that regional residents enjoy today: serviceberries, called "juneberries" in the United States and "saskatoons" in Canada; native plums, the *Prunus americana* species; chokecherries and the larger, sweeter sand cherries; buffalo berries, the basis for an iridescent jelly; gooseberries and their close kin, black or buffalo currants; and red raspberries, for which they had to travel into the Black Hills.[20]

Hunting and foraging, along with farming and ranching, were ways in which Hamilton interacted with and became attached to his environment. Indeed, one of the most compelling themes of his memoir is his affinity for the Great Plains landscape and most especially for his own corner of the plains, which was studded with landmarks laden with meaning. Of the Belle Fourche Valley landscape where he homesteaded, he says little, but of the Cave Hills where he ranched and the butte-bedecked country through which he traveled, he writes fondly.

The Cave Hills, although little-known outside their immediate vicinity, retain an almost mystic attraction for local folk. They are a pair (termed "South Cave Hills" and "North Cave Hills") of large, sandstone-capped, steep-sided, level-topped, pine-forested buttes or tablelands in present-day Harding County, in the northwestern-most part of South Dakota. The name derives from George A. Custer's visit there on his Black Hills expedition of 1874. His party explored a cave on the northeast face of the Cave Hills and named it Ludlow Cave; the buttes thus became known as the Cave Hills. The cave and various rock faces in the hills bear numerous petroglyphs. To early ranchers, the Cave Hills were a magnet because their escarpments furnished shelter for livestock, springs issued from their gulches, and their forests furnished the makings of cabins and fences. Subsequently, the Cave Hills would be withdrawn from settlement in 1903; declared a forest reserve by presidential proclamation in 1904; and incorporated into the national forest system in 1908. Today, the United States Forest Service administers them as part of the Custer National Forest.[21]

Hamilton the rancher navigated a landscape demarcated not by human works but by natural features, including other prominences similar to the Cave Hills and small rivers and creeks that creased the intervening prairies. Visible some twenty miles to the southwest were the East and West Short Pine Hills, and some fifteen miles to the southeast lay the Slim Buttes; each of these areas harbored clusters of ranches just like the Cave Hills. Strewn around and between them were lesser, yet spectacular, buttes such as McKenzie (named for Hamilton's nearest ranch neighbor, Jack McKenzie), Juhala, Thumb, and Pentila. All near the south boundary of Hamilton's ranch headquarters, some of the buttes served as part of his southern fence line. Bull Creek flowed northwest to southeast, dividing the South Cave Hills from the North Cave Hills. Jones Creek, on which the Hamiltons located their ranch, coursed the south face of the South Cave Hills. Both streams were tributaries of the South Fork of the Grand River, the main branch of which ran east about ten miles south of the ranch. Entering the South Fork from the southwest was Clark's Fork, and south of that was the divide into the drainage of the North Fork of the Moreau River. Over to the west some eighteen miles from the ranch, the Little Missouri River made its northward course.[22] Upstream a few miles and on the west bank was Ashcroft, the post office where Hamilton loped over to get his mail. Upstream a few miles more was Camp Crook, where Cave Hills ranchers got their mail until the establishment of Ashcroft post office in 1889.[23]

These landmarks gave Hamilton a powerful sense of place, and destination, as well. At many points in his memoir, he recounts travel along what he calls the old Dickinson freight road from the Belle Fourche Valley to his Cave Hills ranch. This route predated railroads to the Black Hills and was used to haul supplies to the hills from the Northern Pacific Railway at Dickinson in present-day North Dakota. (The railway had designated Dickinson as the forwarding point for Deadwood-bound freight in April 1884.) Starting north from his farm on the old Dickinson freight road, Hamilton counted buttes. First came Mud Buttes, then Two-Top, and after that Macy Butte, just southwest of which was the home, store, and post office of Isaac Macy, veteran of the 139th Illinois Infantry. It was the only house on the route. After that, the East Short Pine Hills became prominent on the western horizon; a western fork of the road Hamilton traveled led to Medora and passed to the west of these hills. On this same route passed stagecoaches of the Marquis de Mores's express line. Leaving the Short Pine Hills behind, Hamilton crossed the valley of the North Fork of the Moreau River.[24]

To a point just north of here, on the divide between the Moreau and Clark's Fork, and perhaps a mile west of present-day Highway 85, Virginia Bill Hamilton paused with his West Virginia bride, Nancy Ellen Showalter Hamilton, as they made their first journey together to the ranch in 1893. He knew she would be impressed with this vantage for her first view of the Cave Hills some twenty-five miles away. More than a century later, the vista from this divide remains sublime. The only human marks on the prairie below are one ranch headquarters, a few Black Angus cows and calves, and here and there a windmill. The Cave Hills are a dark rim on the horizon directly north. Over the viewer's left shoulder rise the East Short Pine Hills, with dark pines distinguishable atop their escarpment. To the east and west, along the face of the divide, rise the many small, bare, steep clay buttes that Hamilton described fondly, each the color of ruddy chalk. The smells of sweet clover and sage are on the wind. Pronghorn flee down the slope. No wonder Virginia Bill came to love the West.

Hamilton's *Dakota* also provides valuable documentation of the history of farming and the farm community in the Belle Fourche River Valley. Homesteading, kinship, water, and local markets were the keys to farming there in the 1870s and 1880s. Hamilton got his homestead by a relinquishment. He paid an earlier settler, Sam Sweet, fifty dollars to vacate in February 1885 and later proved up on the claim on 23 October 1890. His quarter-section homestead comprised three rectangular parcels arrayed along the north side of the Belle Fourche River, some eight miles east of the present-day town of Belle Fourche. It adjoined the site of the present-day village of Fruitdale. His father, Aaron J. Hamilton, and his cousins, William S., Walter S., and Willis G. Hamilton, also proved up on homesteads in the immediate vicinity. Family members proceeded to buy additional parcels of land. The Hamilton clan thus constituted a powerful kinship support network.

The Hamiltons and their neighbors hoped from the beginning of settlement to tap local streams for irrigation. South of the Belle Fourche, the Redwater Irrigation Association diverted water from the Redwater, a river tributary to the Belle Fourche, and irrigated lands in the Belle Fourche Valley. W. H. Hamilton got work digging a ditch for this project, the development of which led to the growth of the village of Minnesela, first seat of Butte County. His parents bought lots in Minnesela, which the Hamiltons considered their home town during their early homesteading days. Irrigation efforts were less successful north of the river, but dryland crops could be raised. Methods were primitive—broadcasting wheat, cutting it with a dropper (predecessor of the binder), handplanting melons as a sod crop. Such farming succeeded, however, because of the voracious markets of nearby Black Hills mining towns.[25]

In the summer of 1890, the Fremont, Elkhorn & Missouri line, part of the Chicago & Northwestern system, building north out of Deadwood arrived at the junction of the Redwater and Belle Fourche rivers, prompting two important developments involving the Hamiltons and other local farmers.[26] First, the railroad decided to bypass Minnesela and build into a new town, Belle Fourche, striking a body blow to the Hamilton's home town of Minnesela. This decision initiated a feud between Belle Fourche and Minnesela that Belle Fourche eventually won, capturing not only the regional trade but also the county seat. The partisans of Minnesela passed down this conflict as an epic legend of heroism (theirs, of course) and of perfidy (that of Seth Bullock, founder of Belle Fourche, and his henchmen). Bullock, friend of Theodore Roosevelt and veteran frontier marshal, had a ranch upstream from Minnesela. The Minneselans reportedly asked Bullock to negotiate for them with the railroad. He proceeded to make a deal to route the railroad to his own new town of Belle Fourche and, after that, engaged in a series of dirty tricks to kill the town of Minnesela.[27]

The sad story of Minnesela proved of little concern to the Hamiltons because of the other important development spurred by the railroad's arrival—a boom in cattle ranching in the territory north of the Black Hills. Ranching here, exploiting the Black Hills meat market, had begun in 1878 when the Deffebach Brothers (John, Dan, and Erasmus—Texans coming out of Colorado) established a ranch on the Belle Fourche River, a mile or so above the present-day town of Belle Fourche. Other big outfits, mainly of Texas origins, followed into the area. Renowned ranches on this range in the early 1880s included the Hash Knife, the E6, the Turkey Track, the Matador, Continental Livestock, Driscoll & Son, and Dickey Brothers. The Hash Knife was the largest, at one time running sixty thousand cattle in the area. Beginning in 1883, the cattlemen shipped cattle from Dickinson, established in 1882, on the Northern Pacific Railway.[28]

Thus, the territory lying between the Black Hills and the Northern Pacific in present-day North Dakota became part of that mythic chapter in the history of the range cattle industry: the great overstocking of the ranges in the 1880s and the disastrous winter of 1886-1887.[29] In the early 1880s, not only were herds of longhorns continuing to arrive from Texas, but also thousands of eastern cattle, backed by hopeful infusions of eastern and British capital, were being shipped west to the range. Many were unloaded from the Northern Pacific at Dickinson and driven south for finishing. By 1884, writes cowboy historian Everett Dale, the livestock industry was at its "peak of prosperity," but it was a dangerous prosperity—"a minor South Sea bubble."[30] In 1885, after President Grover Cleveland ordered cattle cleared from the Cheyenne-Arapaho reservation in the Indian Territory and many had to be sold off, the cattle market slumped. The worst was to come on the northern ranges, however, as the cruel winter of 1886-1887 followed the parching summer of 1886. The pathbreaking Dakota historian Lewis F. Crawford writes, "It seemed that in the winter of '86 and '87, there was a conjunction of all the factors that make for a big loss—overstocked range, thin young cattle, snow crust, extremely cold days and a long period of subnormal temperature, no protection in the way of sheds, and above all no hay to tide the weaker cattle over. From the testimony of ranchers who passed through this trying ordeal, the loss is placed at from 80 to 90 per cent."[31]

Crawford accepted panicky estimates of loss too easily. The mortality rate surely was not so great as he states, but conservative estimates suggest that the Hash Knife alone lost eight thousand head, and the loss was severe enough to cause financial failure for over-capitalized spreads. Widespread liquidation ensued, forcing cattle markets down further. The whole structure of open-range operations did not suddenly collapse but rather died a slow death over the next decade. The big outfits were selling herds cheap. The railroad arrived in Belle Fourche in 1890, providing another option for marketing. Small operators, many of them coming from the ranks of homesteaders and irrigation farmers, took advantage of the situation. By operating more conservatively, using family labor and exchanging with neighbors, they could ride out the hard financial times of the early 1890s and achieve some prosperity by the late 1890s, when the depression ended.[32]

In the middle of this situation were the Hamiltons, coming out of the Belle Fourche River Valley, buying a herd, and moving it to the Cave Hills. Hamilton's autobiography is a textured portrait of how the new breed of stockmen operated. To begin with, they observed the principles of transition all historians of the industry note. First, they put up hay. Hamilton rushed to finish his planting and cultivating on the Belle Fourche each year so that he could get up north and make a good supply of hay. Second, they fenced their range. One of the big appeals of the Cave Hills location was the fact that, with the exception of a few gaps, the rimrock of the hills formed the Hamiltons' north fence line. Their east and west fence lines were shared with neighbors, and even the south line contained some steep buttes that formed part of the barrier. Third, they bred up. Once cowherds were confined, scrub bulls could be excluded, and purebred bulls—mainly Herefords—could be shipped in from the Corn Belt. That is the context for Virginia Bill's humorous story of shooting the amorous scrub bull, Old Diamond Tail (p. 121).

Besides the broad principles of the new style of ranching, Hamilton records the details—scraping snow to expose grass for winter grazing, destinations of the annual drives to market by the Cave Hills "hill-billies," the weights of cattle, and the prices received. He documents the crystallization of a ranching community, its members collaborating for round-ups and branding frolics. He recounts how the breaking of horses calls forth the practice of playing horse-related jokes on one another and how even the antics of a neighbor's pet pig, given run of the house, contribute to camaraderie.

Clearly, Hamilton loved this life, but as his family grew, he and Nancy worried that their children were growing up without the blessings of civilization. Such concern is understandable, given the many references in his narrative to medical problems among family members and acquaintances—frozen legs being amputated, a boy losing his hands to a mower's sickle, sickness again and again, and doctors days away. The Hamiltons made recourse in serious medical situations to Hamilton's cousin, Dr. Hamilton Baker, who lived way over in Sundance, Wyoming. Most of all, though, W. H. and Nancy Hamilton wished to provide a good education for their children.

These concerns and desires led to the move back to the Belle Fourche River Valley, where the Hamiltons were well respected, and where W. H. filled the role of gentleman farmer for a few years. Following his father's death in 1894, Belle Fourche's newly organized chapter of the Grand Army of the Republic had taken the name "A. J. Hamilton Post" in his honor. Cousin Walter was county assessor. W. H. himself served as county commissioner and became known for finishing fine cattle and hogs. Still, this country was not the range he loved. The subsequent move to Missouri, therefore, appears to have been no great letdown. At least he departed with enough money to get the children the education they wanted. He netted three thousand dollars when he sold out his holdings on the Belle Fourche in 1901.[33]

Tidy ranches still ring the South Cave Hills in Harding County, South Dakota. The Cave Hills Road off Highway 85 takes visitors past McKenzie Butte and, as it approaches the southern rimrock of the Cave Hills, to the mailbox of the family who for the past four decades has run essentially the same ranch as Virginia Bill and Jone Hamilton did. Up the drive at ranch headquarters, the woman of the house, an astute local historian, points out where the fence lines ran, where the Hamilton pens for working cattle on the flats were, where Virginia Bill shot Old Diamond Tail. The man of the house, a spiritual heir of Virginia Bill if there ever was one, discourses on the continuing virtues of good saddle horses in an age of all-terrain vehicles. A rumbling drive up an old Forest Service track leads to depressions in the earth that mark the location of the old Hamilton ranch headquarters.

As Virginia Baldwin notes in the Foreword to this reprint, W. H. Hamilton lived a long and full life in Missouri, enjoyed his family, and saw its members achieve the things he had hoped his move back east would bring for them. Haunting, though, are the words he wrote to his son Harold in 1933: "Had it not been to give you children a first class education, I would never have left Dakota."[34]

Notes

1. W. H. Hamilton's "Dakota: An Autobiography of a Cowman" was first published by the South Dakota State Historical Society in Volume 19 of the *South Dakota Historical Collections* (1938): 475-637. Page numbers given in the text of this Introduction refer to the reprint edition that follows.

2. Hamilton, Foreword to typescript copy of "Dakota: An Autobiography of a Cowman," pp. i-iv. The original typescript was preserved within the Hamilton family, and a copy is now on file at the Research and Publishing Program, South Dakota State Historical Society, Pierre. I also want to thank genealogist Larry J. Metz for looking up the Hamilton household in his copy of William A. Marsh, comp., "1880 Census of West Virginia" (from National Archives Microfilm Group T-9, rolls 1411-12).

3. Hamilton, Foreword, p. iv.

4. Ibid., p. xi.

5. Ibid., pp. xvi-xx.

6. Ibid., pp. xx-xxi, xxiv-xxv.

7. Black Hills Half Century Club, *Pioneer Footprints*, 3d ed. (Aberdeen, S.Dak.: North Plains Press, 1973), pp. 67-68. William B. Hamilton and his sons and daughters would later move on to ranches in the Cave Hills, in present-day Bowman County, North Dakota, and in eastern Wyoming. *See also Prairie Tales II* (Bowman, N.Dak.: Bowman County Historical Society, 1989), p. 148.

8. Hamilton, Foreword, p. xxv.

9. Hazel A. Pulling, "History of the Range Cattle Industry of Dakota," *South Dakota Historical Collections* 20 (1940): 471-81, 503-4.

10. Myrle G. Hanson, "History of Harding County, South Dakota, to 1925," *South Dakota Historical Collections* 21 (1942): 2; *Building an Empire: A Historical Booklet on Harding County, South Dakota* (Buffalo, S.Dak.: Buffalo Times-Herald, 1959), p. 5; Jay Trobec, *State of Extremes: Guide to the Wild Weather of South Dakota* (Sioux Falls, S.Dak.: Where's?ware Publishing, 1995), pp. 14-15.

11. United States, Department of Agriculture, Soil Conservation Service, *Soil Survey of Butte County, South Dakota*, 1976, and *Soil Survey of Harding County, South Dakota*, 1988.

12. Doane Robinson, *Doane Robinson's Encyclopedia of South Dakota* (Pierre: By the Author, 1925), p. 334.

13. Works Progress Administration, Federal Writers' Project, *A South Dakota Guide*, American Guide Series (Pierre: South Dakota Guide Commission, 1938), pp. 397-98.

14. Stephen S. Visher, *A Preliminary Report on the Biology of Harding County, Northwestern South Dakota*, South Dakota Geological Survey, Bulletin no. 6 (Pierre, 1914), pp. 90, 92, 96.

15. *Belle Fourche Times*, 23 Jan. 1896.

16. J. Knox Jones, Jr., et al., *Mammals of the Northern Great Plains* (Lincoln: University of Nebraska Press, 1983), pp. 254-56.

17. Hanson, "A History of Harding County," p. 530.

18. Visher, *Biology of Harding County*, pp. 73-74, 88. *See also* Jones, et al., *Mammals of the Northern Great Plains*, pp. 114-16, 332-35; and Paul A. Johnsgard, *Birds of the Great Plains: Breeding Species and Their Distribution* (Lincoln: University of Nebraska Press, 1979), pp. 113-15.

19. Visher, *Biology of Harding County*, pp. 87-88; Jones, et al., *Mammals of the Northern Great Plains*, pp. 320-27, 340-43; Arthur H. Richardson and Lyle E. Petersen, *History and Management of South Dakota Deer*, South Dakota Department of Game, Fish and Parks, Bulletin no. 5 (Pierre, 1974), pp. 1-3.

20. Great Plains Flora Association, *Flora of the Great Plains* (Lawrence: University Press of Kansas, 1986), pp. 355, 368-69, 391-92, 394-96, 402-3, 491-92; Kay Young, *Wild Seasons: Gathering and Cooking Wild Plants of the Great Plains* (Lincoln: University of Nebraska Press, 1993), pp. 75-80, 137-49, 150-56, 161-67, 175-85, 194-200, 273-76.

21. John P. Gries, *Roadside Geology of South Dakota* (Missoula, Mont.: Mountain Press Publishing Co., 1996), pp. 137-39; Edward P. Hogan, *The Geography of South Dakota* (Sioux Falls, S.Dak.: Center for Western Studies, 1995), p. 23; James D. Keyser, "The North Cave Hills," Section 1 in *Rock Art of Western South Dakota*, South Dakota Archaeological Society, Special Publication no. 9 (Sioux Falls, 1984), p. 3; Hanson, "History of Harding County," pp. 553-54.

22. Landscape descriptions and locations in this Introduction rely heavily on my own field work in northwestern South Dakota, guided by quadrangle maps from the United States Bureau of Land Management: Belle Fourche (1983), Redig (1982), and Camp Crook (1982). The *South Dakota Atlas & Gazetteer* (Yarmouth, Maine: DeLorme, 1997) was also helpful. *See* "In Search of Virginia Bill," http://rrnet.com/~plains/bill/index.htm.

23. Alan H. Patera, John S. Gallagher, and Kenneth W. Stach, *South Dakota Post Offices* (Lake Grove, Oreg.: The Depot, 1990), pp. 176-77. Accord-

ing to local residents, the site of old Ashcroft has tumbled into the Little Missouri with a falling bank. Camp Crook is still a viable village.

24. The Butte County Historical Society marked the site of the Macy post office and store on the south bank of the South Fork of the Moreau River. Isaac Macy's grave is a few hundred feet west of the site. For more information on the Medora line, *see* Lewis F. Crawford, *The Medora-Deadwood Stage Line* (Bismarck, N.Dak.: Capital Book Co., 1925).

25. Black Hills Half Century Club, *Pioneer Footprints*, pp. 99-100; W. H. Hamilton homestead patent, Deed Book 5, p. 419, Register of Deeds, Butte County Courthouse, Belle Fourche, S.Dak.; other patent and deed records for all other Hamilton clan members during years 1889-1901, Register of Deeds, Butte County Courthouse; Pat Engebretson, Kay Heck, and Helen Herrett, comps., *A History of Butte County, South Dakota* (Belle Fourche, S.Dak.: Belle Fourche Public Library, 1989), pp. 8-11, 15; Marjorie Benedict Richards, *Minnesela: The City That Never Happened* (Spearfish, S.Dak.: Northern Hills Printing, 1972), p. 7.

26. Hamilton's timing for the railroad's arrival (pp. 48-49) in Belle Fourche is off by one year. The Fremont, Elkhorn, & Missouri Valley sent its first train into the new town in September 1890. *See* Black Hills Half Century Club, *Pioneer Footprints*, p. 125.

27. Engebretson, Heck, and Herrett, *History of Butte County*, pp. 22-24. For an extended memorial to Minnesela, *see* Joe Koller, "Minnesela Days," *South Dakota Historical Collections* 24 (1949): 1-113. The framed plat of Minnesela, inscribed "Vacated 1903," hangs in the local history room of the Belle Fourche Public Library. Hamilton speculates (p. 48) that Bullock was related to Roosevelt, but other sources indicate that the two were just good friends. *See* "Dakota Images: Seth Bullock," *South Dakota History* 20 (Spring 1990): 80.

28. Lewis F. Crawford, *Ranching Days in Dakota and Custer's Black Hills Expedition of 1874* (Baltimore: Wirth Bros., 1950), pp. 11-16; Hanson, "History of Harding County," p. 527.

29. The disaster of the open-range cattle industry and the transition to the more settled practice of smaller outfits is covered in these classic ranching histories: Ernest S. Osgood, *The Day of the Cattleman* (Minneapolis: University of Minnesota Press, 1929), pp. 83-113, 216-58; Edward E. Dale, *The Range Cattle Industry: Ranching on the Great Plains from 1865 to 1925* (Norman: University of Oklahoma Press, 1930), pp. 77-114; and Louis Pelzer, *The Cattlemen's Frontier: A Record of the Trans-Mississippi Cattle Industry from Oxen Trains to Pooling Companies, 1850-1890* (Glendale, Calif.: Arthur H. Clark Co., 1936), pp. 195-217. More specific to the area discussed here is Pulling's "History of the Range Cattle Industry of Dakota," pp. 499-510.

30. Dale, *Range Cattle Industry,* pp. 104-5.
31. Crawford, *Ranching Days in Dakota*, p. 56.
32. Pelzer, *Cattlemen's Frontier*, pp. 213-14; Dale, *Range Cattle Industry*, pp. 110-14; Pulling, "History of the Range Cattle Industry of Dakota," pp. 501-9.
33. *Belle Fourche Times*, 9 Jan. 1896; warranty deed, William H. Hamilton and wife Ellen to Richard Grady, Deed Book 12, p. 225, Register of Deeds, Butte County Courthouse.
34. Hamilton to son [Harold Hamilton], 6 May 1933, typescript copy of "Dakota: An Autobiography of a Cowman," p. 219.

Reprint Note: *Dakota* first appeared in Volume 19 (1938) of *South Dakota Historical Collections*, pp. 475-637. For this publication of the story as a book, photographs and a map have been added. While the old text has not been reset, new page numbers and an index have been added for the convenience of modern readers.

DAKOTA

An
Autobiography
of
a
Cowman

W. H. Hamilton

"Northerly migrations of cattle frontiers to Kansas, to the territories of Wyoming and Montana, and to Nebraska finally compelled the invasion of the Territory of Dakota. But such migrations were hastened by the discoveries of gold in the Black Hills during the seventies which Colonel R. I. Dodge pointed out as a grazing country which 'cannot be surpassed'. Goldseekers, adventurers, freighters, bull-whackers and stage drivers in crossing the southern plains of the territory saw its virgin grasses. Their reports of the ranges and the water as by-products of their stories of the gold mines helped to usher in the pioneer decade of the range cattle industry in the territory."—Dr. Louis Pelzer in "The Cattlemen's Frontier."

DAKOTA
AN AUTOBIOGRAPHY OF A COWMAN

W. H. HAMILTON

I was reared on the same farm that my father was. I left West Virginia the winter of 1884, first going to Mahaska County, Iowa, where I worked for a farmer until about the first of May. Then I got it into my head to get out on the frontier, but did not have the price, so I went as far west as my money would carry me. I had to stay over Sunday in Lincoln, Nebraska, and had my watch and money stolen that night in a rooming house. But there was a "fiver" stuck in a vest pocket the thief missed. I used it and got as far as Western, Nebraska, a small town in the center of the state, and got a job with a German farmer at $20.00 per month with board and bed. The last of May my parents, having sold out in West Virginia, came there and were fortunate enough to rent a small farm with crop already put in, so we could all be together on week ends. I worked for the same man all summer. He was a good honest man, but expected a man to earn his wages. We were in the field at work by six o'clock in the morning and came in as the sun went down. I always got an hour at noon, but what time I was not eating my dinner I spent pumping water for five horses, ninety to a hundred hogs, and twenty head of cattle from a ninety foot well. But I was young and tough and did not mind, tho no one had to rock me to sleep when I did get to bed.

I worked on for him until he had his corn husked, and he had one hundred acres of it. I plowed it over three times and I do not believe that he helped me more than six days altogether. He hauled the corn to town two miles away to pay me my summer's wages at thirteen cents a bushel, and it seemed like it took a lot of it.

After the corn was husked and winter set in, there was no more work to be done, so I got the wanderlust, and on December 16, 1884, I started for Deadwood, taking the train at Fairbury and going to Sidney, Nebraska. There I took a stage coach three hundred miles to Deadwood. There was a heavy storm on and the stage was held at Sidney until it would moderate. So on the morning of the 19th the stage driver came in the hotel and said he would try to go as far as he could, but he said it was going to be a tough trip and those who did not absolutely have to go had better wait awhile until it moderated.

The stage line was owned by a company whose name I do not recall, and it honored any railroad ticket. So I had bought my ticket at Fairbury to Deadwood, Dakota, by way of Sidney, for $50.00. And since I had my transportation paid, I did not carry any more money than I thought would last me through. I had been at the hotel two days and they surely made one pay for all he got. I saw that I had better move at the first chance, so I said I was going if the stage went.

There was a soldier boy stationed at Fort Robinson who had been down to Missouri on furlough, and his time was out, so he said he had to go. And lastly, there was an old lady, a Mrs. Miller, whose home was in Rapid City and who said she was used to the cold and blizzard, so she was going. The assistant superintendent of the line decided to go as far as Fort Robinson, and the driver went to make up the party of five.

So about 9:00 A. M. Dec. 19th, we pulled out. It was 35 degrees below zero that morning, but there was no wind to speak of. The snow was pretty deep, and the wind the day before had drifted and packed it very badly. The team of four horses with the old cumbersome coach made slow going. The country was not entirely level, but rolling for a considerable distance north of Sidney. We had not gone far until the windows were all frosted over, so we couldn't see much country except when we got hung in a snow drift and got out to help lighten the load. Sometimes I helped shovel snow, but not so the soldier boy. I believe he would rather have sat there and frozen than work. But the superintendent was not afraid of a shovel. He rode on top with the driver all the time to help him drive and find the road. His name was J. M. Strawther. The stage company had what they called stations all along where they changed teams. These stations were from ten to twenty miles apart, depending on where they could get water and make hay for the stock. There was a man at each station to care for the stock and always have them ready to go on. He was known as the stock-tender. He had a one room shack, usually of logs, about 14 by 16 feet, and just high enough to allow a tall man to stand straight. The roof was made of boards, covered with six inches of dirt. The stables were about the same, but larger. Oats were kept in the house in sacks, and these came in handy for beds in case of company.

I do not know how many station houses we passed the first twenty-four hours, but I remember we crossed the North Platte River the night of the 20th about midnight, with the wind blowing and the snow a-flying. Strawther had asked the last stocktender how cold it was and he said it was 30 below at dusk.

We had been pretty lucky so far in getting something to eat, as the stocktenders wanted to stand well with Strawther. They usually had plenty of meat of some kind, potatoes, and baking powder bread stirred to a stiff batter and dropped into a pan with a spoon, then baked in a quick oven. I thought those were the best meals I ever ate, but they cost from 'six bits' to a dollar.

We had gone only a short distance from the Platte until the road or trail went between two hills, and the wind had filled that low ground so full of snow the horses could not get through, much less pull the stage. Well, the two men on top got down and shovelled for awhile, then drove up and shovelled some more. They had to keep the team up close because the snow blew in nearly as fast as they shovelled it out. After about two hours I got cold and got out to help. I think that was about the coldest wind I ever felt, but I got to work, and after awhile, I got warmed up, but both the other fellows were about all in. The soldier was nearly frozen, but he sat inside and shivered and would not shovel. Finally we got through and by shovelling many other places, got to the next station just after noon, got warm and filled, but Strawther and the driver were "tuckered", so they decided to stay there until the wind went down. The wind didn't go down, but got worse, and by night it was a regular blizzard, so we stayed there that night, having lots of buffalo robes, grain sacks, blankets, and plenty of wood to keep us fairly comfortable. We made a bed for Mrs. Miller in one corner and she said she slept fine. I slept some, but not fine, but we all felt pretty well. The wind had gone down, but it was cloudy and very cold, so we started about nine in the morning, having fresh horses, but they didn't stay fresh very long. The snow was packed so it made terrible pulling, and I am sure we did not make more than two miles per hour, having to shovel in all the low places, and getting the team down many times.

It was almost night when we got to the next station and we were all played out. I think that was the first time in my life I was ever really hungry, and I ate my seventy-five cents worth that night. The driver said he could go no farther that night, and I was glad of it. I would much rather stay in where it was warm, even if I did have to stay up and fire the stove. We got through the night fairly well and started on our way next morning, but not rejoicing. We were all pretty badly frostbitten, ears, nose and fingers, and all very sore. We were in a rough and broken country now, and as long as the road followed a ridge, it was fairly good travelling, but we had to do much shovelling in places, crossing creeks and ravines. But we got to the next station by a little after noon, got something to eat, a change of horses, and went on after dark, after a little while getting to a station called Pumpkin Creek, where we stopped and ate a snack. After eating, we hitched up about midnight to start, and just as we started the team was cold and hard to manage, giving the driver all he could do. There was an old well covered with boards nearby, and the horses pulled across it. Down went a front wheel, throwing the driver off the top, and all of us inside down in one corner in a pile. Part of the team was balky, and when the sudden pull came, they stopped, and a good thing it was for us too, for if they had gotten a good start, they might well have strewed us all over the landscape. We had to get logs and poles, and anything we could to pry and lift to get out, but we got out, and nobody was hurt. We got going, and about 10:00 A. M. the next day, we got to Fort Robinson, where we were able to get a square meal at an eating house. There our soldier and Strawther left us. We got a new driver and traded our coach for a pair of bob-sleds with a wagon box on top. Our new driver said he had been over the road only once before, and he was not much acquainted with the landmarks, but thought he could make it. We started about 3:00 P. M., with the road visible only in places. As it began to get dark, we came to a ranch near the road, and the driver said if the rancher would let us, we would stay there overnight. The fellow said yes, so we put up for the night, had a good supper, good beds, and the first chance I had to remove my clothes since I left Sidney.

The next morning (Christmas) we started about seven. It was clear and still, but very cold, with ten miles to go to Big Cottonwood, the next station. We made better time with the sled and arrived there about half past nine that morning, changed horses, and had a good warming up. The stocktender said he did not know what he would do for something to eat, as he was out of everything but potatoes. He said he had ordered meat, flour, and all kinds of groceries, but we met the stage he had ordered by away north of the Platte River and it was no telling when it would get back.

We started on about ten o'clock, and the snow was very deep. I saw a cloudy haze hanging back in the northwest, and in about an hour after we started, it struck us. The air was so full of snow we could hardly breathe and as fast as the sled left a track, it was filled level. We could scarcely see the lead horses. The country was pretty level, with a few draws, or dry creeks here and there, and when we came to one of those, we had to shovel to get the team across. We drove all day and at about sundown the wind went down until it was perfectly calm, and I saw a light in the distance.

So we began to drive toward it and it was not long until we drove up to a station, and imagine how surprised we were to find it was Big Cottonwood, where we changed horses that morning!

Well, we went in and the stocktender boiled us a big pot of potatoes, on which we made a meal, and they tasted real good, too. He had lots of sacked oats in the house, from which we made beds, used buffalo robes for blankets, and got through the night fairly well.

I froze my feet rather badly that day, and found some trouble in getting my boots on next morning, but finally did so, and was ready for my share of 'taters. The boy found some bacon grease, and so we changed to fried potatoes. He also located some coffee and sugar.

It was cloudy, but the wind was not blowing much, so we started once more. We had travelled about an hour when the wind started to blow, getting worse every minute. By ten o'clock it was as bad as it was the day before. Sometime that day, when the team was about played out, the driver and I left it a short distance to shovel a road across a dry creek, and out of a little clump of brush jumped a jackrabbit. It stopped about a rod from us and I drew my wonderful .32 six gun and slew him. About that time I looked up to see the team running off with the old lady in the sled all covered up with robes. The driver said to never mind, they wouldn't go far, and they didn't, for they tried to cross the creek near us and the leaders got down with the hindmost team piling in on them in a bunch. We got them straightened out after some time and were ready to go again. The driver said to get that rabbit as we might need it, so I threw it in the sled. Well, it got still again that evening, and at dark we saw a light, so we whipped up to hurry and get to the station, and lo and behold, it was the same station we started from that morning. We had been travelling in a circle for two days!

But we had meat for supper, even though it was too tough to stick a fork in. The broth helped the potatoes somewhat, and I kept a fire going all that night until the rabbit was pretty well done by morning. We had a good breakfast, all things considered. The weather had moderated some during the night. It was not so cold, and almost clear, but I told the driver I was staying right there until we ate all that boy's potatoes, or until the weather got better.

During the runaway the day before, Mrs. Miller was covered up so well with blankets and robes she never knew we had a runaway.

After I decided to wait for better weather, the driver said he would wait for the next stage to come through before starting, as it was his second trip and he was not too sure of the road when he couldn't see the track. We stayed there all day but the wind did not blow any. It was cloudy until about the middle of the afternoon, when it cleared and the sun came out. About four in the afternoon a sled came in from the north, with three passengers. One of them was Tom McMaster, and one Mack, the saddler, from Deadwood, with whom I later became well acquainted. I do not remember the third man's name. McMaster was going to San Francisco to see his brother Sam, one of the principal stockholders in the Homestake Mining Company, and who died before spring. Mack, the saddler, was going out on business. I later bought my first Western saddle from him and gave $55.00 for it.

Well, as the wind had not blown any all day and it was the time of the full moon, the driver said he could take the backtrack and make it to the next station, Willow Grove, which was seventeen miles away. The track was plain and the night was bright and still, and I believe one could have heard that sled squeak for two miles. We made pretty good time, only having to stop to shovel through a few drifts where it was too deep for the team. We could see a long distance, and I saw some buttes off to the left I thought were not more than two miles away, but the driver assured me they were much farther. I did my first driving with four lines that night, when the driver's hands would get cold, and he said I was the best he ever saw for a beginner;

but he didn't fool me any. I rather enjoyed the drive that night, it was so much more pleasant than what we had been experiencing.

We got to Willow Grove about midnight. The stocktender came out to help us put away the team, and the first thing I asked him was if he had plenty of grub. He said yes, and I said to go and get some of it ready to eat and we would take care of the team. We first got our lady passenger out of her bed and into the house, and soon had the team eating hay. In a very short time the boy had hot bread, steak, fried potatoes, and good old black coffee ready, and I have known ever since that a healthy young man cannot kill himself eating, or I would not be here to tell you this. I am sure I never saw so much grub stowed away by three people in so short a time.

That old lady was a wonder. She never complained about anything, was always cheerful and full of fun. She had gone to the Black Hills in '76 and was made of the kind of material that the frontier settler had to be to survive.

We slept until about eight the next morning and started on before noon. It was cold, but not stormy. We did not drive any more by night, but lay over with stocktenders. We still had to shovel lots in low places, and to cross ravines and dry creeks. We traded our bobsleds for the coach again before we got to the hills, taking the coach of the south bound party left in exchange at Snake Creek. We were now getting close to the hills and the streams were open. As we crossed the stream from Hot Springs, it came up almost to the bottom of the coach. Mrs. Miller had a tin cup and reached out and got us a drink as we crossed the creek. It was almost milk-warm.

We crossed Rapid Creek just before getting to Rapid City on the evening of Dec. 29. We were so played out with frozen feet, hands, ears, and noses that the driver said he was not going on to Deadwood that night if he lost his job by laying over. I put up at a hotel, had a good bed, and got to take off my clothes once more, making twice that I slept like a white man since I had left Sidney.

The next morning was a very cold one, 40 below zero, with considerable wind, but we were on our way by eight o'clock with three other passengers on board. Mrs. Miller had stopped in Rapid City. The roads were drifted very badly, and we skirted the hills, keeping on the north and east sides. We changed horses at Blackhawk and Sturgis and came through Crook City (now Whitewood) and on into Deadwood, arriving there at six in the evening—a very homesick, discouraged tenderfoot, with his feet frozen too badly to get anything on but overshoes, among entire strangers, and with $1.75 in his jeans.

* * * *

While I am resting my frozen feet in Deadwood, I shall dip back into family history briefly.

In 1847, two of my father's brothers, William and Henry, thought Virginia was too tame for them, so they started west and came to Scotland County, Missouri. Uncle William bought a farm near the town of Memphis (Mo.), but Uncle Henry, like his father, a great hunter, did not take to farming, but put in most of his time hunting and roving over the frontier.

In the spring of '49 a caravan was formed that was going across the plains to California. He and another man were appointed scouts and hunters for them. They had mostly ox-teams, with about one hundred men in the party, besides women and children. They had many thrilling adventures, including several brushes with the Indians. Buffalo and other game were plentiful, so they had very little trouble in supplying meat. I do not remember how long they were in making the trip, but I recall that my uncle died of mountain fever in 1855.

Uncle William married and settled down on his farm. When the Civil War came on, he joined the Federal army and served four years, being with Sherman on his march to the sea. After the war, he engaged in farming and stockraising, until he reared his family. He had six boys, all grown to manhood, whom he knew would be wanting homes and land of their own soon, so he concluded he would sell and go farther west where land could be had cheaply.

In the spring of '82 he sold and moved to Sully county, Dakota, about 25 miles from Pierre, where he and two of his sons pre-empted a quarter section each, living there a year. But water was very scarce and hard to get, so they proved up on their land by paying $1.25 per acre and got their patents. In the fall of '83 they took their livestock, machinery, and houshold goods, by wagon across the prairie westward to the Black Hills, then went out twenty-five miles north of Deadwood, locating on the Belle Fourche River.

In the summer of '84, while living in Nebraska, my father thought he would pay his brother William a visit. He had not seem him since he had left Virginia in '47, so in July he went to Deadwood in three days, the season making the fast trip possible. I was eleven in going over the same territory. He made the acquaintance of two men in Deadwood who had much to do with my destiny on reaching there, although I did not know of them, never having heard my father speak of them.

My father came back to Nebraska in September and was not much impressed with Dakota. He said it was a good place to make money, but was a poor place for a civilized being.

* * * *

I had eaten lunch in Crook City, so, as my finances were almost exhausted, I decided not to have any supper. While I was there in the hotel office, a young man came in and asked me if I came in on the night stage from Sidney. When I said I had, he began asking me about the trip, and as I was glad to have someone to talk to, I opened up and said plenty. He wanted to know what kind of accommodations we got on the line, and what kind of work stock they had. I told him I did not think much of the workstock or drivers, that the company had a few good horses at each end of the line, but that the majority were no good, would not pull, and that I considered them old rundown horses good for nothing except wolf-feed. I did not know that the young man was a reporter and a booster for the Pierre Stage Line. After he got all he wanted, he went out, and I went to bed to sleep the sleep of the just.

Next morning, when I came down, the clerk handed me the paper and pointed to a column headed "Hamilton's Experience". I read it over and was very sorry I had said so much, for the article contained all I had told the reporter. But it was all true and I could not unsay it.

That morning after breakfast, I was sitting in the lobby of the hotel when another young man came in and asked the clerk if a young fellow was stopping there by the name of Hamilton. He said yes, and pointed me out to him. He came over to me, offered me his hand, and said: "My name is Rice. Are you a son of A. J. Hamilton?" I answered, "I am". "Well, I know your father," he said. "I met him last summer at his brother's ranch out in the Belle Fourche Valley, and when I read of your experience, in this morning's paper, I thought I would look up you. My brother-in-law, W. L. Hamilton and I are partners in law. He is sick, and his wife and children are back in Missouri visiting this winter. I must be at the office through the day, and I do not like to leave him alone. I thought I might persuade you to make your home with us for awhile. We are batching. Can you cook?" I said, "I might boil water without burning it, but that would be about all." But he said, "If you will come and stay with us, we will manage the cooking."

I thought he was an angel from heaven, and I was not long in accepting the offer. I gathered up my few belongings, paid my bill, and hobbled after Mr. Rice, who had taken my valise. After paying for my night's lodging, breakfast, and a much needed shave, I had "two-bits" left in my pocket.

We followed the one street for a short distance, and then started up steps, right up the hillside. We continued upward, still climbing steps, for the distance of about three blocks, to where they lived. There I met W. L. Hamilton, a tall, spare man, with a full dark beard, piercing brown eyes, but a pleasant, mild-spoken man, and one of the shrewdest lawyers of the Black Hills. He had been elected prosecuting attorney of Lawrence Couuty, of which Deadwood was the county seat, in '84. He had gone to the hills from Memphis, Missouri, for his health, as he had lung troublc, of which he died some years later. He was circuit judge for one term after he had served one term as county attorney.

Things went along smoothly for me, and by the help of Hamilton and Rice, I picked up some ideas about cooking. They were both not only smart men, but were pleasant and agreeable to be with, and I learned many things from them about the life and customs of that country of value to me in later years.

I will say in passing that Mr. Hamilton was not related to me insofar as we could ever trace, although he was born in Philippi, W. Va., only fifteen miles from where I was born and reared. His parents had moved to Missouri when he was a small boy.

The winter was a very severe one. It kept snowing and blowing, and out on the prairie the snow was drifted so badly it was impossible to travel with a team. Stage lines were blocked, and people in Deadwood and the other hill towns were in a bad way to get hay and feed for their teams and milk cows. Hay was selling on the streets for $50.00 to $60.00 per ton. Potatoes were ten cents a pound, butter a dollar, eggs seventy-five cents to a dollar a dozen, corn five cents per pound, while flour was only $5.00 per barrel, as there was a fine roller mill in Deadwood, and they had laid in a big supply of wheat in the fall. There was another good mill at Crook City in the northern edge of the hills, and another at Minnesela, twenty-five miles north of Deadwood.

After my feet got better, so I could get my boots on, I would go downtown to the office of Hamilton and Rice. One morning Rice said to be down to the office by ten and I could see the Homestake Co. place its month's output of gold in the bank. It was to be in a brick, and as the office was just over the bank, I could get a look at the brick from the window; and you may bet I was there. About half past ten, a coach drove up with driver and a guard on top. When the stage stopped, a guard with two six-shooters got out, and his hands were on his guns. Then two men came out carrying the gold between them, and out came another guard, also armed with two six-guns. The man on top had a Winchester rifle. That was the first and only gold brick I ever saw.

I wrote a letter to my parents the night I got to Deadwood, and I also sent them a paper a day or so later, but they got no word from me until some time in February. You can imagine their uneasiness when they kept reading of the terrible storms in the northwest, and got no word from their wandering boy. I kept watching for a word, and also a little cash, from them.

As I got so I could get around better, Mr. Rice (or Greene, I shall call him) would ask me to go out with him for a walk and see the sights of the town for a short time. About every third or fourth door on Main Street was a saloon, and most always in the back was a gambling den, besides gambling tables in the same room with the bar. There were all kinds of games going on. They all had their little scales for weighing the gold dust. Those saloons were crowded every night with miners, cowboys, professional gamblers, gunmen, outlaws, and every kind of character imaginable. Some had their guns lying in front of them, some in their sidebreast holsters, some hanging from hips, but all had them, and had them in easy reach. And the strangest thing to me was, there was no noise, everything perfectly still, scarcely any talking, everybody alert and paying strict attention to business, each man watching the other. There was a dance hall down on Main Street, called the 'Gem Theater'. I think it was the hardest place I ever stepped into. That was the only dance hall I was ever in where everyone danced with his six-gun on. In later years I was at and took part in many dances at halls and private homes, but we always shed our guns when we went on the dance floor.

I have read many books on Western life and the life of the cowboy, and they almost invariably make the cowboy a rowdy and a ruffian. I want to say right now, I spent eighteen years of my life working with cowboys, and I found them to be just the opposite. The cowboy is always a gentleman where he is supposed to be such. You can depend on him to stand by you to the last ditch, as a friend. To be sure, he will gamble, but he will be honest with it. Most of them will drink some, but they respect the other fellow's rights. When he falls in with a rough bunch, he is ready to be as rough as any of them.

I told Greene I did not care to visit the Gem anymore. I was wanting to get in touch with my uncle and family, but there was no way of getting word to them, as the mail could not go out to Minnesela, their post office; and if mail got out there, they could not get to the office to get it, as they lived six miles down the river and had a very rough country to pass through, with snow drifted in places six to eight feet deep. If they should shovel it out as they went to the office, it would be drifted full as they came back.

While I was staying with lawyer Hamilton, Greene asked me one morning if I would like to go over to the court-house with him. Court was in session. I said I would. After we were there awhile, a mining case was called. It seemed as though there was a dispute as to the ownership of the mining claim. A man by the name of Joe Moore was attorney for one party, and a Mr. Frawley was counsel for the other. Greene told me afterwards that they were good friends and had worked together on many cases, but today they were on opposite sides and it seemed to be an interesting case. I was enjoying it immensely, when Frawley called Moore a liar and Moore knocked him down. The Judge said, "I fine you gentlemen $25.00 each." Frawley raised up on one elbow and shouted, "Don't pay him, Joe. Don't pay the old devil a d—— cent." I never learned if the judge collected the fines or not.

I was getting very anxious now to get out to my uncle's especially when I saw a few loads of hay on the streets and knew they must have come from the prairie north of Deadwood. So in a few days I was talking to a man with hay for sale and I asked him where he cut the hay. He said on the Belle Fourche River. I asked him if he knew a family by the name of Hamilton, and he said he certainly did, that they lived near him. I asked him if there would be a chance to go out to my uncle's with him. He said "Sure, if you can put up with the accommodations." I said I thought I could put up with anything any other tenderfoot could, so he said, "All right, you be here at seven in the morning and we will go." He then told me his name was Frank Brian, and I hurried off to the office of Hamilton and Rice to tell them of my good luck. They said that they knew him, that he was a horseman, and a near neighbor of my uncle's.

By this time, Mr. Hamilton was much better and at his office most every day. This was three weeks after I had landed in Deadwood, and my feet were entirely well. I had a new growth of skin on nose, cheeks and ears, and was feeling fine, but had heard nothing from home. I did not sleep much that night for fear I would oversleep and miss my chance to go out.

When I got up in the morning it was warm, and water was running everywhere. A warm wind, known as a Chinook, was blowing from the southwest, and was melting the snow very fast. I hustled around, got down to the livery stable on time, and we got started soon afterward. We had about five miles to go to get out of the hills and timber. Then we came to Centennial Prairie, so called because the first settler on this prairie north of the Black Hills, was located in the fall of 1876, the year of the centennial celebration at Philadelphia.

By the time we got out on the prairie, the snow was melted off where the wind had blown it thin, and in many places the ground was entirely bare. The road led on down False Bottom Creek for about eight or ten miles, then we pulled across a stretch of rough, broken country, covered with scrub oak (called "crooked oak" in that part of the country), for four or five miles. This brought us to the prairie that finally leads down to the Belle Fourche River. Just as we got through the scrub timber, the prairie gumbo began and lasted almost to the river. For the benefit of those who do not know much about gumbo, I will say that it is the most sticky soil "what am." I have gotten stalled going downhill with an empty wagon, and that is a bad predicament to be in, for you can neither unload nor back up.

As we started down the slope after getting through the timber, I said I believed I would walk a way. Frank remarked that I had better stay on the wagon. But I thought I wanted to walk, so I got off. I had not gone far until I saw I was in bad, but Frank had started up and was away in the lead. It was not thawed enough to roll on the wagon wheel, but the gumbo certainly did stick to my feet. I tried to run, but I could hardly lift my feet, there was nothing with which to scrape the mud off, and had I scraped it off, I could not have gone three steps until it would have been as bad as ever. So when Frank had had all the fun he wanted, and thought the tenderfoot had learned a lesson, he waited for me to come up. I got on the wagon, and after I got breath enough I asked, "What kind of mud is this?" He laughed at me awhile and then said, "That is gumbo, and the worst in this part of the country."

We got to the river, and Frank drove right in on the ice, not stopping to try it. It had two or three inches of water on top of it from melted snow and looked rather dangerous to me, but he told me I need not be afraid of ice on the Belle Fourche from December to March. We stopped at his place just after crossing the river. I was for going right on, but Frank said no, that he would get some dinner first and then he would go over with me. He got a good dinner ready in a very short time (he being a professional chef, and always cooked for a cow company during summer on the roundup.) After dinner we walked over to Uncle Will's, and they were "some surprised" to see me. One of the boys had gone for the mail that day, and had not gotten back. I had never seen any of the family except the youngest boy, who had been in Missouri when I visited my relatives in and around Memphis in the spring of '84. He did not go to Dakota until that September. That evening my cousin Willis came back from the post office and had the letter I had written the first of January. I think I got to Uncle's January 24.

They were all well and glad to see me, and it is useless to say I was glad to be with them. My cousin Alden, the youngest boy, had cut his foot very badly a few days before I got out to the ranch, and was getting around on crutches. One of the older boys, Walter, had located a homestead on Owl Creek, about six miles from his father. My uncle was not living on his homestead, but on a rented place adjoining it. He had not yet built a house on his own land.

Soon after I got to Uncle's, he and I began hauling lumber for his house . As he had a good sized family, he would have to have considerable room. There were three boys and two girls, and the parents. My aunt was a large, fine looking woman, much younger than Uncle, always cheerful and good humored, and always ready for a joke. Uncle and the boys were milking a good many cows that winter, and after the roads got passable, sold the butter up in the hills and got a good price for it . I went with him to Deadwood soon after I got to the ranch. We took two loads of corn, for which he got five cents per pound, and he had something over 100 pounds of butter, for which he received seventy five cents a pound.

We always took our beds when planning to be gone over night. He had several pairs of buffalo robes and blankets, one robe underneath with the flesh side down, then our blankets, then a robe on top. I have kept very comfortable in zero weather out in the open thusly. Getting up of mornings is what takes grit.

I helped Uncle haul the lumber for his house, because he seemed to think he had to be along on such expeditions and I much preferred such trips to staying home milking and caring for the stock. We hauled the lumber from the Black Hills, in south of where Whitewood now is. It took two days to make the trip. We always stayed at the saw-mill overnight and came home with our loads next day.

Uncle was a very quiet, mild tempered man, scarcely ever getting excited or out of humor under the most trying conditions. I lived with him and near him for many years, and I never saw him the least bit excited but once, and I have seen him in some pretty trying places. The range cattle were quite troublesome at times and would break in and eat with the cows. One morning we boys thought we would give them a scare with the dogs. Uncle had an old dog he had brought from Missouri, and he thought lots of him, although he was not worth two-bits. We tried to set him after the cattle and he would not go a step, but when a young dog they had started in to chase the cattle, then old Sport flew in and nailed the young dog. They went at it teeth and toenails and the young dog was giving Sport what he deserved. Uncle was in the corral milking, and hollered "Boys, part those dogs." But we wanted to see the good work go on, so we hid in the barn and pretended not to hear. Directly Uncle came running down to the scene with a bucket of milk in one hand and a big stick in the other, ran up to the dogs, and blazed away with his club, but hit the wrong dog and laid old Sport out stiff. Well, now things were doing around there for awhile, and I thought for a time all the young Hamiltons round about would be disfigured for life, but after a little bit, Sport got to his feet and made a crooked path to the house. The boys told me afterwards "nothing but a dog-fight ever excited pa."

The chinook wind took all the snow off except the drifts, but it only lasted one day and night, and then it got colder than ever. Lots of mornings it was 35 to 40 below. I think 42 below zero was the coldest it got, and that was on the 30th of January. We had no more snow to speak of until late in April. In the meantime, I got four or five letters from home. They were written at different times, but I got them all in a bunch.

We got our wood across the river in the scrub-oaks. It would take two of the boys all day to get a load, and it was hard work at that. On a clear morning one could hear the old wagon squeak for two miles.

There was a man by the name of Sam Sweet who had located a homestead just a half mile west of Uncle's claim, and he had torn down and moved an eight room house to his place. He had also built a shack on the place, and had broken six acres of sod. He was sick of ranching, and wanted to sell me his lumber, relinquish his claim, and let me file on it. He said he would take $150.00 and step right out of the whole thing. I had left some money with my father, and I told him I would take it as soon as I could get the money from home.

It was now March 1, and the ice was breaking up in the river. Everything was going fine. Uncle had hired a couple of carpenters, and we boys were helping them, trying to get the house up so they could move in before they started farming. I had rented a farm adjoining my Uncle's on the east, from Sam Wheeler, he to furnish team, seed, and tools, and give me half of the crop; so I was a full-fledged farmer. Sometime in March I got some money from home, went to Deadwood, paid Mr. Sweet, and filed on the land as a homestead. I had a hard time to make the officials believe I was of age, having to call my uncle in to swear I was twenty-one. I looked like a kid of sixteen or seventeen.

The weather was mild for the time of year so far north, and we were rushing the work on Uncle's house as much as possible. We had gotten the doors and windows on the last trip to Deadwood. The man Uncle had rented from wanted to come back and get ready to begin the spring work. He and his wife had been running a rooming house in Lead City. Grass was beginning to get green, and the meadowlarks were coming back north. About the last week in March we moved in the new house, not yet done, but we thought the downstairs to be usable, and we boys could use the upstairs as sleeping quarters. I had already begun sowing wheat, putting it in broadcast, then plowing it under with a twelve inch plow. We liked to do it as soon as the frost was out of the ground, plowing it under to a depth of about two inches. At that depth, two horses could turn three acres per day. I had my wheat all in by the middle of April, sowing the six acres that were already broken on my claim. But I had to harrow that in, as it was only second year sod, and had not rotted yet. The tools we used were very primitive, old wooden harrows and wooden beamed plows. We did not know what a disc was. I harrowed two days on the six acres, and then only had it about half covered, but there was something to follow shortly which put it under well, and I raised forty bushels of wheat to the acre.

I had already sowed my oats on the rented land, and finished sowing wheat about April 20. The night of the 22nd it began to rain, and by morning it was snowing and blowing so one couldn't see a team 100 feet away. It was not very cold, just below freezing, but the wind was terrible. It would blow the snow in at a keyhole and make a good-sized drift where there was no fire. Uncle had some shoats in a pen with one side open, and they were soon drifted under. So we had to get a team out, get the hogs into a wagon, and take them to a bank-barn on the place I had rented. That was a real job, for a team just would not face the storm. Finally we had to leave the team at the barn with the hogs. The weather had been so nice, and the grass was growing so well that the stockmen and cowboys had gathered all the range cattle that had drifted across the river during the winter, and had thrown them back north on the open range for the summer. As the river farms were all fenced, the cattle drifted south and east until they came to these fences, and then went along the fence east, right by Uncle's house; and there was a continuous stream all day, one right after the other, in single file with heads almost to the ground. There must have been several thousand of them, for they went by all day. About a mile east of Uncle's house, there was a big "draw" which emptied into the river, and on each side, where it emptied in, the banks were fifty or sixty feet high, straight up and down. Those cattle, walking so close after each other, just walked over that bank until they formed a bridge of cow-flesh. I never saw as many dead cattle in all my life as there were in that pile. The storm lasted from the night of the 22nd to the morning of the 24th, and if it had not drifted, the snow would have been more than two feet deep. The sun came out brightly on the 24th, and as it was not very cold, the snow was all gone in two or three days except in the big drifts. Our oats and wheat came right up and grass was growing, but the ground was very wet. The storm and soggy ground were mighty hard on cattle, as many of them were very thin and weak from the severe winter they had just passed through.

As soon as the ground was dry again, I commenced plowing for corn. I wanted to put out all I could, for I had a letter from my father saying he had decided to come to Dakota and bring a small bunch of cattle. As spring opened up, the settlers began to come to the valley, and desirable land was soon taken. New improvements could be seen going up every day. I put out a good garden, and broke out a piece of sod for melons, for they did better on sod-land and it was not necessary to work them, for no weeds grew on first-year sod.

My parents started from the little town of Western, Nebraska, on May 10. In the company were father and mother, sister and brother, and two boys by the name of Jake and Lee Ridgeway, who had come from W. Va. in order to come on to Dakota with them. There was also a young man from Nebraska named Jim Applegate, who came along with them. They had two teams, one horse, one oxen, and about thirty head of grade Shorthorn cows. They came northwest to Sidney, and then north by the route I had come the winter before. Both wagons were covered, and they had a good big tent. They travelled very slowly and had to "lay over" some on account of young calves. They had fifteen hens which furnished eggs all the way on the trip, and they had plenty of milk to use. Father would not travel on Sunday, saying that he always rested at home on Sunday, and he would do the same while moving. I asked my mother if the chickens were not a lot of trouble, but she said not, that when they camped of evenings, they just opened the coops and they came out, scratched around, caught bugs, ate their suppers, and when roosting time came, they went back into their coops.

They had pretty good weather most of the way. Mother said she thought she walked more than half the way. She would walk on ahead of the teams and wait for them to come up. When she left W. Va., she was in poor health, and her friends and relatives thought they would never see her again. But she said she was not on the road a week until she began to feel better and the farther she went, the better she felt, and when they arrived at my ranch July 2, her cough had left her, and I don't remember of her being sick a day until a week before her death April 1924 at the age of 86.

I was certainly glad to see them all. They were so tanned they looked like a bunch of Indians. I had my corn about laid by and I had a fine garden. With my small cabin, a tent and the two wagon covers, we managed to make out on living quarters until father could look around for a location. I had lumber enough, with doors and windows, for a good eight room house.

My claim was in an L-shape and adjoining it north and east was a fine quarter section that a man had entered in 1880, had plowed about two acres, had gone away, and had not been heard of since. So I asked my father why he did not contest this claim, for I did not think the man would ever come back to claim or improve it. After considerable pressure from my uncle and myself, he decided to do it. The law in such cases was that one could file a contest claim, and at the end of six months, after giving notice through a newspaper, if the former claimant had not proved his right to the land, then the contestant could file for it.

It came harvest time and I had no reaper, but a man near me had one of those old Buckeye droppers and did not have team enough to pull it, or hands to bind after it. So Uncle and I went in with him. We furnished the binders and half the team. Two of my cousins, my brother, and I were doing the binding, and we got along fine, but with a good quick team in heavy grain, there was no time for play.

One day while binding on my wheat, I pulled in just after the machine passed me, so I was not more than three sheaves behind the dropper. I picked up my sheaf, and as it came up under my arm, I felt something cold on my hand, and just then I heard the rattle of a snake. I think I scattered that wheat over more ground than it had grown on, and there not more than three feet away was a big prairie rattler, coiled up and ready for business. Always after that, when I would hear one rattle, I would feel the same coldness on my hand. I afterwards ran many narrow escapes, but they never affected me quite like that one did.

During the late summer my brother and I dug a well on my claim and struck good soft water at thirty feet. We also broke considerable sod, so as to have land for wheat the next year. The young men who came with my parents found work nearby with ranchers, and we were together nearly every Sunday.

Families were coming in with children, and they were talking about school. By fall, there were enough children to demand a school, and a district was organized. But we did not have a schoolhouse. My father, uncle, and a man by the name of May, were appointed directors. There was but one applicant as teacher, and that was Lee Ridgeway, one of the boys who came from W. Va. The directors rented a room from a widow, whose ranch was next to mine. We were to have six months of school—three beginning Sept. 1, and three in the spring, starting April 1.

After Sept. 1, father decided to build on his claim, and wanted to get the house up before winter set in. I let him have the lumber I got with my claim, and he hired a man by the name of Jutt to build it, or rather, to oversee the building of it. He was an old man, and had consumed lots of bad liquor in his time, but knew his business. He would not agree to come out from town to work unless father would furnish him with one quart of gin per week. He just took one good swallow before each meal. If the gin ran out he would not hit a lick until it was forthcoming. So the trade was made—he was to get $1.50 per day, and his quart of appetizer each week. My brother and I were pretty handy with tools, so he laid out the work and we did most of the actual labor. We got along fine, and by the last of October, moved in the downstairs of the six room house, using the upstairs in which to sleep. The frame was sided, weatherboarded, and ceiled inside. No one ever plastered in that day, as the plaster would not hold on account of the terrible winds.

We cut all the corn and hauled it into the corral, and built a makeshift barn and sheds by digging back in the bluff at the junction of the river bottom and prairie land. We dug back into this bluff about twenty feet, set posts hauled from the hills, with pine poles for stringers, covered with brush gotten from the river, mostly willows, then covered that with slough hay. As we were never bothered with rain while we needed shelter, it did not need to be waterproof.

We got our feed all in, other work done, and had some time to hunt besides. There were lots of grouse and sagehens, and plenty of jack-rabbits. They came to our corn in the corral, and on a bright night one could kill all the rabbits he could carry. As we were on the northern edge of the settlement, by going out four or five miles, we could get all the antelope we wanted, so we were never in need of meat.

In September, Dr. Hamilton Baker, a cousin of ours, and has brother-in-law John Bonafield, came out from W. Va. Dr. Baker was a surgeon and graduated from Johns Hopkins in 1880. He rented an office in Minnesela, and was the first doctor to locate in the Belle Fourche valley. He put in a small stock of drugs and was the only doctor and druggist nearer us than Deadwood. He said afterwards he would have starved had it not been for setting broken bones and cutting bullets out of the cowboys, as no one ever got sick. "Doc" got himself a good team of ponies and a buckboard, the fastest mode of travel in that day. Their families did not come out until the spring of '86. John made his home with first one and then another of his relatives until then.

One day the latter part of October, John and my brother took a team of ponies and buckboard and went out to get some antelope. They went over on Owl creek, about where Orman Dam now is. They got no antelope, but came back with a full load of sagehens and jack-rabbits. The next day they went on to Deadwood with them and sold every one for fifty cents apiece.

We had been milking a good many cows all fall after we weaned the calves, as nearly all the cows father brought with him were "broke to milk." Butter had a ready sale at fifty cents a pound in the mining towns. As there was no railroad closer than Pierre, everything had to be freighted in by ox and mule team, usually twelve or thirteen yoke of cattle, or six or eight mule teams to a heavy wagon, with a trail wagon. The advantage of a trailer was that if one got hung on a hill, the trail could be dropped and gone after later. It was amazing how those bull-whackers could turn the corners in the narrow streets of Deadwood. It looked as though it would be difficult for me to handle four horses in such quarters. Things were very high in price because of the freighting expense. No change less than twenty-five cent pieces were used until after the railroad came to the hills.

We had lots of cold weather the winter of '85 and '86, but very little snow, and cattle could graze all the time if the wind was not too high for them. We had shelter for most all of our stock, so we got them through in pretty good shape. In looking after our cattle and going to a few dances through the winter, my brother and I got pretty well acquainted with the cowboys and ranchers all through the valley.

One little incident I might mention here was the corner on coal-oil in the winter of '85. After the freighting season was over in the fall, some fellows slipped around to the merchants of the hills and bought up all the oil before anyone saw what was up. We had been paying $2.50 per case (ten gallons) and when they got it all, they put it up to $1.00 per gallon. We decided to boycott them, and you cannot imagine the different ways one can find to make a light when it becomes necessary. We got along fine, because mother, for some reason, had brought her old candle molds with her from W. Va. and we not only used them, but loaned them to the neighborhood. And in this way, we beat the trust.

One of our substantial ranchers was to be married in April. He was a Dane, and a fellow everyone liked. He had a good many cattle and horses, as well as the best ranch on the river, so we were all looking forward to the big time when Jim Larsen would bring his wife home. For we not only knew that he would have the best dance of the season, but also knew all the girls and married ladies of the valley would be there. And more than that, we knew old reliable Jim would have the best of everything to eat and drink, especially the latter.

Well, the ice had gone out of the river and the ground was working fine by the middle of March. We did not put out much small grain, sowing wheat on what we had broken the year before. But we rented a bottom-land farm joining my place and put out about seventy acres of corn, and expected to break out considerable sod for corn, which would require no cultivation.

The schoolteacher boarded with my parents, and we boys were together on all social occasions. The big dance was to come off the 5th of April. Jim had a big house and it was arranged so we could dance in three rooms to the same music. We all gathered early, and there were cowboys there from as far as twenty miles around. The women folks brought all kinds of cake, pie, doughnuts, and everything good to eat. They had a good big room for the wraps and small children, and right on the table with the grub was most any kind of drink a body would want, and everybody had a tip-top time. I never heard a cussword or angry remark from anybody the whole night, and all went home happy.

Well, with the dance and marrying all over, we buckled

down to work, finished sowing oats, and had our plowing for corn all done by the middle of May. We set to planting soon after, as we had to plant our corn by hand. Horse planters had not yet gotten to Dakota. We harrowed the ground well, then marked it two ways, and planted in the cross, so we could plow it each way.

In May, Dr. Baker's and John Bonafield's family and with them two young men, Billie Burgoyne and Latham Wolfe, boyhood chums of mine, came out from W. Va. After his wife and children came out, John rented the Minnesela Hotel and ran it for the next two years.

After we got our corn planted, we broke some more sod on my place, and about twenty acres on father's. No one showed up to claim his quarter, so he filed a homestead on it, and sold my brother "Jone" and me a two-third interest in the cattle and horses, taking our notes for it, as our cash was very low.

We had no hard rains, but did have some nice showers that started everything to growing, and grass was coming along fine.

I was supposed to be living on my claim. I did sleep there all the time, but I boarded with my parents more than at home. The well we dug was as close to father's house as it was to mine, and as we had been very busy, we made the well answer for both houses and the barn. The cattle watered at the river. We hauled pitchpine posts from the hills and put fences around both ranches.

The district decided to build a schoolhouse. I gave an acre of ground, where the town of Fruitdale now stands, and the house was built during the summer of '86, all ready for the fall term of school. There were then about thirty pupils in the district.

It was getting along in June and was very hot for the time of year. It was also getting pretty dry. We had plowed our corn over once, and it was looking fine; we had branded our cattle and horses with our company brand, and we had

had a good calf crop. One acre of melons had been put in on sod, and they were doing well, the weather was getting pretty dry for small grain, and grass was not growing.

About that time, Texas cattle began pouring in by the hundred thousand. The three-V, Hash-knife, B&B, 101, and Turkey-track, or E-6, were all running them in thick and fast, and they were eating everything they came to. Billie Moses was foreman for the Three-V, Russ Wilson ran the Hash-knife, Ed Lemmon the B&B, and Joe Driskill the E-6. Things looked pretty black for the small stockman and also for the rancher. If it kept dry and hot, it looked like the man who had water for irrigation was the only one sitting pretty.

It kept on dry, and on July 4 (on Sunday, I remember it so well) 1886, it was the hottest day I ever saw in any country in which it has been my pleasure to live. The wind blew a gale all day, and it felt like it came off a red hot stove. The only way we could have any comfort was by hanging wet blankets over a hoisted window, and they would dry out in a very few minutes. Well, the next day when we looked over our corn and grain fields, it made us sick. Our hopes were all blasted. Our corn which had looked so promising was lying flat on the ground, as dry as fodder. It was plain that nothing could be raised that season, even if it rained plenty from that time on until fall. So everybody began looking around to get something to do to get through the coming winter.

I knew of a man who had an irrigated ranch ajoining Minnesela. He had a good many cattle and horses, and he wanted a man to care for them. I went to see him at once and he still needed a man. He looked me over and said; "Young man, I have gathered these cattle and horses from different localities and they are going to be hard to hold, with hot weather and short grass making it harder. Do you think you are equal to the occasion?"

"How many horses can you furnish me to ride?" I asked.

"As many as you will need," he answered.

I said, "I will do my best, and I think I can do it."

"You are a very young looking boy, but I will try you. When can you begin work?" he asked.

I said "Right now," so we went over to the hotel and he said to John Bonafield, "Give this young fellow room and board and charge it to me until further notice."

So I was hired at $50.00 per month and board, and I was "some pleased." I was going to make good if I had to work day and night.

If I remember rightly, it was Thursday, July 8. I went home the next Sunday to take my horse home and tell the folks what I was doing.

He gave me a good string of horses, and the man he had temporarily stayed the rest of that week to help me get a line on the stock and the range they were supposed to be kept on.

My employer was Azby A. Chouteau from St. Louis, and a descendant of the first settler of that city. His father was a very wealthy man and had given the boy all the money he wanted and the right to do as he pleased. He had an irrigated farm where he raised lots of alfalfa, owned the hotel building, a big up-to-date flour mill, a big livery stable, and besides his range stock, had some good trotting-bred horses. He was a very nice man to work for as long as one did right.

It never rained a drop from the middle of June on, and having had no hard rains all spring, with many hot winds, there was nothing raised on the dry ranches at all. One acre of watermelons was the only thing that matured on our land. They did not get very large, but were the sweetest I ever tasted. My brother hauled a few loads to the hills and did well with them, getting enough to buy flour and groceries for the winter.

The grass dried up, and with so many range cattle on it, by fall there was nothing outside the fences. We had not pastured our homesteads, and the grass was fairly good there, so the cattle did very well up to mid-December. We had to have some hay from somewhere, so my brother and uncle, and one of his boys, went out northeast about thirty-five miles where there did not seem to be so many cattle. They found some pretty good hay, although it was a long way to haul it. The three of them camped and put up hay for about six weeks, got up almost a hundred tons of pretty fair hay, and hauled it in during the fall and early winter. They would go out one day and return the next. It was a slow process, but better than doing without.

The boss and I got along fine. He turned the horses inside after he got his oats harvested, and I had only the cattle to care for. I had a string of good horses and stayed right on the job, and nothing got away that was turned over to me. Some had gotten away before I was hired.

When winter came, we turned the cattle inside. I supposed. my job was at an end, but the boss said he could use me in the mill until it froze up. So the next morning I went to work in the flour mill.

People who never lived on the frontier must not get it into their heads that all the hardships and privations were borne by the men alone. The women played just as big a part in the great undertaking as the men, and in some instances, greater. While I was away at work, my brother out making hay, my uncle and all his boys away, my aunt and the two girls ran the ranch, milked a number of cows, and kept the home fires burning. My father and sister looked after our cattle milked the cows, and when my father made his weekly trip to the hills with butter and eggs, he took the produce for my aunt also. Mother and sister did the work the two days a week he was gone, besides keeping cases on the herd. Man knows not what he can or will do until put to the test.

I became acquainted with a young cowboy by the name of Charley Holbrook the summer of '86. He ate at the same table with me all that summer. He was a well educated young man, reared in Philadelphia, but wanted to see the frontier. His parents were dead, but he had one sister. He was working for a cowman on a ranch on the Little Missouri River, near where Camp Crook now is. In March the man wanted to send a few Shorthorn bulls across the head of Clark's Fork to another ranch he owned about twenty miles away. The weather had been fine, and on the morning of the 20th, the cook fixed up a small lunch and Charley started. The boss went with him to get them to driving well, and then turned back. The day was not cold, but somewhat cloudy. Charley had worked all over that country the summer before and knew it well. There was no ranch between the two, and none for many miles to the northeast. He said that about ten in the morning the wind began to blow, it turned colder, and that by noon it began to snow. Finally a blizzard developed and by the middle of the afternoon, he could hardly see the cattle he was driving. But he kept going, and when night came, he turned the cattle loose and began to ride toward the ranch, as he thought, and rode all night. The next morning it was not so bad, but still snowing, and he could see nothing that looked familiar at all. So he rode all day, and all that night. The next morning the wind had gone down and the sun came up bright and clear, but everything was covered with snow and he had no idea where he was. Before noon he was so snow-blind he could not open his eyes. He was in rough country and there was good feed for his horse under the snow. He was walking all the time now, but after he got blind, he got on his horse and turned his head loose, thinking he might take him somewhere. But it seemed to him the horse travelled in a circle all day and night. The next day he let the horse stop and graze often. The snow was melting and he could get water wherever he wanted. Finally, he said, he could stand it no longer on the horse, got down and unsaddled him, found a place where the snow was off, wrapped himself up in his saddle blankets to die, and was asleep in a minute.

When he awoke it was day, his blindness had left him, his horse was gone, and his feet were frozen solid. He crawled up on a little hill nearby, and not a mile north he saw the E6 Ranch, where he worked the summer before.

This was sixty miles northeast of where he had started the morning of the twentieth.

He started to crawl down the slope, when some of the boys saw him, first thinking it was a bear and were about to take a pot-shot at him, but made out with glasses that it was a man. They hurried out, took him to the house and fed him some broth, then got him into a buckboard as soon as he could stand it, and started for Minnesela, more than one hundred miles away. He said he did not know much about what was going on. In twenty-four hours they had him in town. Dr. Baker said there was no way to save his life but to amputate his legs, and this he did right away. Charley was all summer getting over the terrible exposure—it was March 26 when the boys picked him up and started to town with him.

This man had lived through all that and was still lively and cheerful. He said the only thing that made him feel blue was that he knew he could never ride the free and open range again.

During the summer several families settled in our little county seat. A family by the name of Lee came from our old neighborhood in W. Va., bought lots and built a house. There were six in the family. Jake, the father, got a good team and hauled freight from Deadwood to supply the two general stores, one owned by Ed Bowman, the other by an old lady by the name of Isabel. She carried anything from farm machinery down to a paper of pins, if she could only find it when she wanted it.

The work at the mill was not hard, but we worked pretty long hours. A cowboy by the name of Dan Roberts—Kid Roberts, he was called—ran a saloon in the town, and it was a great loafing place for the boys. The cow-season being over, the boys had to have some place to gamble and drink and spend their hard-earned money.

There were lots of boys who came up the trail from Texas in the summer of '86 and two of them I remember well were Joe and Bob Highshaw. Joe was a quiet, easy-going, pleasant fellow. Bob was just the opposite, and very quarrelsome when drinking and gambling.

One evening when I was going to supper after work, I passed the saloon on the way to the hotel, and as I did so, I saw Bob and Billy Shultz playing cards at a table near the door. There was no one else in the saloon except the bartender, "Ducks," as the boys called him. I saw that the boys were drinking and were getting quarrelsome. I went on to supper, and before I was through eating, Ducks came rushing in and yelled, "Bob has killed Billy."

Joe jumped up from the table and ran out with some of the other boys. As I was a little late getting to supper, I finished my meal before I went down.

When I got there, Doc Baker had pronounced Billy dead. He had been killed instantly, shot through the head, and it was a clear case of murder, as Billy did not have his gun on. The sheriff, Harry Stevens, was there and asking lots of questions, but Bob was gone and was never heard of afterwards.

The next afternoon we buried Billy out on the prairie near the town, the first in the plot that became the Minnesela graveyard.

We had already had one blizzard, and by the first of December it was getting to be real winter. The mill, being run by water power, froze up, and I went home about Dec. 10.

Brother Jone had been running a snow plow made of 2 by 12 inch timbers, twelve feet long. By pulling this over the prairie with a team, the grass was exposed, and the cattle were doing very well on it. We were saving our hay for future use. The horses were doing well, as they would paw the snow away.

I had to now go to living on my claim in earnest, as I was not allowed to be off it more than six months at any one time, and I had been away that long. My mother gave me some pointers on how to cook certain things, and I made out fairly well until I tried cooking my first rice.

I always liked rice, and I thought I would cook enough so I could have some cold the next meal or so. I had five pounds, so I put about half of it in a good sized stew pan, after washing it well, and set it back on the stove to soak until morning. The next morning it looked like there was more, yes much more, than the night before. I built a fire, poured more water on the rice, and went back to bed until the house warmed up a little. Directly I heard a sizzling noise, looked out, and saw my rice running over. I got up and put half of it in another vessel, and by the time I got my clothes on, it was running over again. Before I got that rice cooked, I had everything full except the waterbucket.

The winter had set in about right by Dec. 1. It wasn't so cold, but there was lots of snow. The range cattle were beginning to drift badly. There was lots of wind from the northwest, and cattle were already coming through from Wyoming and Montana. We kept busy plowing snow and saving all the feed we could. We had good shelter, as father and brother had built a shed 100 square feet. This was sided on three sides, and covered with poles, willows, and slough hay, with poles on top for weight.

The railroad had built as far as Buffalo Gap in the summer of '86, and we decided to go down and get a load of corn. About Dec. 20, father and Uncle Will took a team apiece and started. It was 80 miles to the Gap. The snow was deep, and the thermometer stood well below zero all the time, but they could make ranches to stop at nearly every night. They also had a good bed and camp outfit, should they be caught out. They made the trip down fine in about three days, got their corn, and started back. But they met a storm the first day out, and it was so strong from the northwest they could not face it. They stopped at a ranch for the rest of the day and night. Next morning it was better, so they pulled out, but had lots of snow shoveling, made slow progress, but kept at it each day, and got home the 28th, having spent Christmas on the road, but we all felt good that they were back safely, and had a good load of corn each.

After they got back, the weather got much worse—

just one storm after another until Jan. 3. That morning when we got up, there was a Chinook wind from the southwest, with the thermometer standing almost sixty above. The snow was melting fast, and it looked like our troubles were over, with prospects of it being gone in a short time. But before noon the wind changed to the northwest and it began to get cold. By night it was down almost to zero and the next morning it was 16 below, with a stiff wind blowing. The snow had such a crust a man could walk on it, and stock could scarcely travel. We had to begin feeding our hay, for we could not remove the crust with our snow-plow.

Thousands of cattle had already drifted in on the river, and they had nothing to eat except willows and young cottonwood. Before spring there was not a twig left within reach. The range cattle began dying by the hundreds. I saw range cattle that had drifted in from the northwest after the crust had come on, with their legs entirely raw to their knees.

The last two days of January and the first of February were the worst three days of blizzard I ever saw. The air was so full of fine snow a barn fifty feet away could not be seen. There was so much static electricity that if one touched a stove with an iron poker, the sparks would fly and it would shock the holder like a battery was wired up with it. Just at dusk of the second day the wind stopped blowing from the northwest for about two minutes, and it was so still the direction of the wind could not be made out. Then it started in from the northeast and gave us 24 hours more like the 48 from the northwest.

We had some late calves which were about to freeze, so we caught them and put them in a dugout we were not using, and by so doing, saved all of them.

That was the last blizzard of the winter, but it about finished the cattle business. It stayed very cold all through February, but there was not much fresh snow. The last day of the month, the wind began blowing from the southwest, with a rising temperature, and by the third day the water began to run on top of the ice on the river. By the tenth day, the ice rose and began to break up and gorge. What cattle that were able, began to move back on the range. Snow-water, coming down out of the Black Hills, put the river up and the heavy ice would gorge, then push up huge cakes out on the bottomlands. Some would have huge rocks frozen in them which must have weighed tons. When the ice melted, the rocks were left far out from the river.

Well, we got most of our cattle through, although some of them were very thin, but at that we were thankful we got out so well. Spring opened right up and we were sowing wheat by March 20. Others were not so fortunate as we, and the cattle business was sorely hit. Everyone had lost heavily, and some outfits were practically wiped out. The Turkey-track and E6 had shipped in 27,000 head the summer of '86, and they only rounded up 250 head of them the next summer. The native cattle did not die so badly as the late shipped-in-ones, and there was about 75% loss on native cattle. Consequently, everyone wanted to sell, and no one wanted to buy. I have found that that is a good time to buy, but it takes a lot of grit to do it. Ed Bowman, a Minnesela merchant, had brought in a small bunch of good Hereford cows the summer of '86, and although he had bought lots of feed, he had lost heavily. He had become thoroughly disgusted with cattle and wanted to sell. Father had some money, and I had most of my summer's wages, so we bought the cows for about half what they were worth. He also had a small bunch of Oregon mares, which we bought, and moved them all out to the ranch in May.

One day during the spring a very amusing thing happened. One of my neighbors owned a big raw-boned steer with large horns and a bob-tail. I always wanted to laugh every time I saw him. This steer persisted in running with our milk cows. I had driven him to the range herd several times, but he was always back by the next morning.

My well was a short distance east of my shack, and not far from my father's house, so we both used it. It had a good top on it, but was not fenced. We drew water with a windlass and a five-gallon oil can attached to a thirty foot rope. The windlass was not fastened to the top of the well, but rested on two forks.

One morning while building a fire in my cookstove, I heard a commotion among the cows. The old steer had been rubbing around the windlass and had gotten the rope fastened on his big horns in such a way that the can was standing on top of his head, bottom up, and he was going across the prairie at a forty-mile gait with about fifteen cows after him. That windlass was striking the ground about every twenty feet, and he bawled about every time it hit. It stayed with him for a quarter of a mile, and I had to go after the windlass before I could get water for breakfast.

It did not stop the steer from running with the cows, but I never saw him rubbing around the well again.

The summer of '87 not far off found my old boss asking me to work for him again. I told him I could not get away before June. He said that was all right, and added that he wanted me to go on the roundup, to start about the 10th, the cattle being too weak to handle before that time. We got our grain in and considerable sod broken by June 1.

Going on the roundup meant that I had to get myself a bed, and I felt rather important as I went about this errand. I went to work for the boss when the spring roundup started. He had made arrangements with Billy Moses, who was foreman of the Three-V, for me to go with one of his wagons. He gave me the same horses I rode the summer before, and they were good ones.

As I was a new man on the range, I was not supposed to do any of the fine work, being treated something like a freshman is treated by the upper classmen at college—"seen but not heard." I had some good friends among the boys, and by keeping my mouth shut and eyes open, I got along very well. We had lots of rain, and 'though it made everything look fine, it also made the work very slow and disagreeable. Some days, we could not move at all, but we had to hold the herds day and night, just the same. It was rather trying to crawl out of a good warm bed and get out in a wet stormy night to take our turn on guard. We had no tent in which to roll our beds, just right on the ground. If a fellow didn't have a good tarpaulin, it was just too bad, that's all.

I always pitied our night "horse wrangler," for he had a tough time. When we were on the move, he rode in the bed wagon and caught what sleep he could.

Almost any pony will buck if he is saddled up after a cold wet night. But if it had not been for the fun of watching the boys get dumped occasionally, I think we would all have gotten the blues and quit.

I remember one big fat boy particularly, named Nick Kefler, like myself, a tenderfoot. He had a little black horse that would pitch him over his head almost every morning. Jack Talbot, our wagon boss, said, "Nick, when you get on Nig, rare back, and he won't pitch you over his head."

So the next time it came Nig's turn, Nick got on and Nig commenced.

Jack was nearby and yelled, "Rare back, Nick, rare back." But Nick "rared back" as Nig went up, and fell backwards in the mud.

Nick jumped up, mud all over, shook both fists at Jack, and howled, "Now, there is one of your d—— rare-backs."

When it came to branding, I was allowed to "rassle" calves, but the roping was done by the experts, and they did not always rope them by the legs—sometimes around the neck—then bring them to the branding fire. It was no small job to get hold of a jumping, bucking 300-lb. calf, and lay him down, but after a little practice, I could do it with any of the boys. It was not done altogether by strength, but also by knowing how.

About the middle of June it began to get hot, and, well, say, anyone who has never been in the north in mosquito time knows nothing about them. You simply could not breathe without something to protect your face. I have seen them so thick on horses I could not tell their color, and sometimes they would get so bad the range horses would all leave the country, going out facing the wind.

In the spring of '87, a man by the name of Kirkpatrick, father-in-law of Walter Hamilton, drove to Dakota in a wagon, and brought along a young stallion to sell. We bought him to use in breeding the Oregon mares we had obtained. He was sired by a Percheron horse, and was from a purebred Morgan mare, and I think was the best built and most powerful horse of his size I ever saw. He weighed about 1400 pounds. From this cross, we raised some of the best horses in the country.

I did not stay on the roundup all summer, but came back to Minnesela to look after the cattle and horses for my boss about August 1, boarding at the Hotel again. I quit work in September and went home to help cut the corn and do the fall work.

About that time we were all made sad by the death of Billy Richmond—"Scotty"—as he was known. He had been sick at one of our neighbor's home all summer. Dr. Baker had been giving him medical aid, but had said from the start that he could not cure him, for he had "Stomach trouble," or what would now be called cancer. We took turns staying with him of nights and did all we could for him. He told us where he wanted to be buried, on top of a butte just across the river, and he said, "Boys, bury me deep enough so the coyotes won't dig me up." Everybody liked Scotty. He had only one fault, and that was drink. He would drink up everything he made. He said he had no relatives in this country, and he did not want his people in Scotland to know where he was. So we made up enough to bury him decently, and laid him to rest on top of the butte. That was the first death in the valley.

The summer of '87 was a good season, and everybody raised lots of melons of all kinds. One of my near neighbors had a wonderful crop of them, and he hauled them to the towns in the hills.

He had one of the ugliest horses I ever saw in color, formation, and disposition. He was what we called a milk-and-cider color, with a white face, all four legs white almost to his body, and had a humped back. He would kick at everything that came in reach of him.

One day neighbor Brian was driving along the street in Deadwood, (and that was the time of the high bicycle with a big and a little wheel) when a lady came riding along by the wagon, and Brian said, "Be careful, lady, don't go so near that horse."

She kept right on going, and said in a rather insulting tone, "Oh, I'll not scare your old team."

Just then old Hoggy reached out with his left hind leg and shoved it through the spokes of the big wheel, and as his leg came back, the bike stayed with it. When Hoggy got done kicking, Brian said that the bicycle looked like it had gone through a rock-crusher.

I asked Brian if he paid the woman for the bicycle, and he said he never saw her after he got Hoggy and the bicycle separated.

After we got our fall work done, and feed all in the corral, brother and I thought we would take a short antelope hunt. So we rigged up a wagon and went out north about twenty-five miles for a week's hunt. We went near what is known as "Two-top," two high buttes so close to one another they looked like they had grown up out of the prairie together. The weather was fine, just a little frosty of nights, but clear and warm during the day. But so many had been hunting that the antelope were very wild and scarce. We managed to get a small load, however. We would kill them and dress them with the hide left on, keeping them in the shade, and they would cure out and keep well for many days. After we had hunted three days, we pulled for home, getting there about ten at night. Father then took a fresh team and went on to Deadwood with all but two which we kept to eat. He sold them all right away for four and five dollars each.

We were not very well satisfied with our hunt, and after putting our cattle inside the pasture, we thought we would try going farther out, so on Oct. 20, we started North again, going out the old Dickinson freight road, camped near Two-top the first night, and went on to Macy the next day. Macy was the only house we saw from the time we left the sight of home until we got back. Jim Macy kept the post office there, and cattlemen scattered through that part of the country got their mail there once a week. The office was supplied by a buck-board from Minnesela to Camp Crook, a village on the Little Missouri River, where General Crook made camp when he was after Sitting Bull, following the massacre of General Custer and his army. Camp Crook is eighty-five miles north of Minnesela. Macy is on the south Moreau River. Just after crossing the river, one road goes north to Medora, on the Northern Pacific Railroad, the other going northeast, on the east side of the Short Pine Hills, to Dickinson, North Dakota. We camped north of the river, and next morning took the northeast road.

We had not seen many antelope, so we kept moving along north and east that day and in the evening were near the head of north Moreau. It clouded up and began to mist, so we decided to pull over west into the hills. Then, in case it got cold, we would have plenty of good pine wood. We found a good camping place in a little cove where we were sheltered from the wind, and put up our tent, and picketed our horses on good grass.

We had killed two antelope, so we had meat for supper. After supper, the sprinkling continued, but it was not cold. A short while after dark, we went to bed. I awoke sometime in the night to find the wind blowing a gale, and it appeared much colder, but I pulled the "tarp" over my head and went back to sleep. When I awoke next morning, a first class blizzard was on. I hurried out and took the team down into a canyon out of the wind, strapped their blankets in place, and got back into the tent as quickly as possible. I couldn't see fifty yards, and it was terribly cold.

Well, there we were, fully eighty-five miles from home, with no winter clothes. Neither of us had overshoes or overcoats. We were in for some tough times, but it was of no use to give up. It stormed all day but late in the evening it got still, cleared off, and the sun went down brightly, but the cold was fierce. We were not very hungry for supper, for we had kept up a fire in the tent all day and kept roasting and eating antelope most of the time.

We were undecided on which way to go to get out of there. The way we came in was rough, and we knew the drifts would be bad, particularly so as we had no shovel. Neither of us had been in that part of the country before, but we were sure the road to Camp Crook was west of us. We had seen a roundup trail which led across the hills, and following it would take us over to the Crook road.

So after a good breakfast next morning, we started on that route. The team seemed anxious to get out of that part of the country, and I know we were. The drifts were not so bad but that we could get through them by hunting the right places, so about ten in the morning we came into the Crook road and started south. Not long after we struck the road, a cowboy overtook us on horseback. I asked him where he hailed from. He said Camp Crook. I asked him how he crossed the river, and he told me on the ice. So you know it was cold to freeze the river hard enough in one night to hold up a horse.

One of us would ride and drive as long as he could stand it, and then we would trade places and run behind the wagon to warm up. We never stopped to eat anything until we got to Macy that night, and then Jone did not eat, for when he got warm, his feet hurt him so badly it made him sick.

The next morning he got some sacks and wrapped his feet in them, as he could not get his boots on. I let him have all the clothes I could spare, for he could not walk.

I walked almost all day and we made the fifty miles home by ten that night.

That was the last hunt either of us ever took, except to hunt and be home by nightfall. Jone's feet bothered him all that winter and he suffered with them the next spring. In ten days the snow was all gone and the weather was fine until after Christmas.

Bill McMaster, the Irish rancher of whom I have spoken before, had a man holding about five hundred head of cattle up on Owl Creek that fall, as the feed was poor near home. He had a tent, and herded them so as to keep them together, intending to put them into the pasture later. But when the storm came, he went into his tent and let them all get away.

So a few days after we had gotten home, and Jone had gotten so he could hobble around pretty well, Mac came down and wanted him to come and help his man gather up the cattle. Jone first said he could not go, but Mac pleaded so hard he finally said he would try it if he were given a string of good gentle horses. Mac said, "Sur-r-r-e" and you know every horse I have, and you can have your pick and name your own price." So he went up in a day or two. He had worked for Mac before, and he knew that he would be expected to bring in at least a few cattle every day. When they began to gather and turn them in, they at first could get a good bunch every day. Each day they were to keep count and report to Mac at night the number turned in. After a few days they could not find them so easily, so if they got, say ten head, they would turn in seven or eight and leave the others outside the fence. Then if they failed to find any next day, they turned in those left out the day before and counted them. Mac was satisfied if only two were counted.

He worked until sometime in December and got about all the missing cattle. I do not remember what Mac gave him, but I know he paid him well.

I said when I got to Deadwood in '84 I would never go out of the Hills until a railroad was built in, and by the fall of '87, the Fremont, Elkhorn, and Missouri Valley had built to Whitewood, thirty-five miles from our ranch, and I was beginning to want to see the girl I left behind me. So I began to plan to go back to W. Va., and I wanted to spend Christmas there. Jone told me to go, that they could make it all right without me. We had plenty of feed to carry our stock through, and we had quit milking so many cows. There wasn't much left to do, so I got ready, and I think it was Dec. 20 when I put an extra shirt or two in a valise and Jone and I started for Whitewood before daylight, as he wanted to come back the same day. We got over there by noon, and before I got my ticket I ran into Jake Lee. He said, "Wait until tomorrow, and we'll all go with you." So he rushed around and disposed of what little stuff he had. He had been working on the railroad. After the work shut down, he sold his team, and was about ready to go back to W. Va. We pulled out the next evening by way of Chicago, and I got to spend Christmas with my girl and my relatives.

I made my headquarters with Uncle Jim Hamilton and family. He had one boy, Oran, near my own age, and he also had two saddles with two or three good horses to go with them. Oran and I kept them on the go most of the time. We always managed to get in and to bed by daylight. It seemed as though everyone wanted to give me a good time. I got back a little too late to take in the apple-cuttings, but there were lots of other kinds of parties, and protracted meetings were just in full blast, and a young man who has never been to a protracted meeting in the mountains of W. Va. has just about missed half his life. But I finally got the measles and lost almost a full week right in the best of the season. I had an uncle, an aunt, and a bunch of cousins over the mountain on Cheat River near St. George and we went over and spent a week with them.

But time soon passed, and before I knew it, it was March 1, almost time to be heading home. My girl and I had talked the matter over pretty well, and we came to the conclusion that we had better let things rest for awhile.

She had a good job teaching school, and had a state certificate that was good for about eight more years. I was considerably in debt yet even though I did have a homestead and some cattle and horses, so the future did not look too encouraging. I don't think she wanted to give up a forty-dollar job for a ten-dollar man anyway. It was decided, then, I would go back to Dakota alone.

A cousin of mine, John Dennison, and a cousin of his, Albert Clarkson, thought they would like to go home with me. I talked to their parents about it, and they said they did not object if the boys wanted to go, but some of their aunts got very angry at me for persuading the boys to go away out there among the Indians and outlaws. Nevertheless, the boys got ready, and we started for Whitewood March 12. When we arrived there, no one was there to meet us. Next morning we struck out across the country and walked it, leaving our luggage behind. We made it in home that evening, three very tired boys, but happy to be home.

The weather was nice and the ranchers were beginning to think about farming. Meadowlarks were singing, and the grass was starting up. The winter had not been a hard one and the cattle had come through fine.

I got work for both the boys with a neighbor across the river. He irrigated his half section of land, and had another half-section on the north side, adjoining my father's. He raised lots of alfalfa and had work for the boys all summer.

We put all our broken ground in wheat and oats, and then broke out considerable more that spring.

A horseman, living just to the north of us, wanted twenty-five to thirty head of horses broken that summer— some to work, some to ride. Jone and I took the job, and it was a tough one, as some of the horses were five or six years old, were big strong fellows, and as wild as a horse could get. The big ones we broke to work, and the ones not weighing over a thousand pounds, to ride. Those saddlers certainly had plenty of action. I let Jone do most of the riding, as he was a good rider and liked it. I was not so good, and I know I did not like it.

The man had a good big round corral, out on the open prairie, with no fence to bother, once outside it. It was a good place to hitch up or to ride them the first two or three times. We would rope and pull their feet from under them, put a halter on, and if they were to be worked, we put a "double-U" on their front feet before we let them up. With this, one could pull their feet from under them and throw them with one hand, yet it did not keep them from walking. If they got bad, a pull on the rope brought them to their knees. On the ones we rode, we put the halter on and blindfolded them while they were down, then let them up. Not one horse in fifty will move while blinded. Then we saddled them, put a "hackamore" on instead of the halter, got on, pulled off the blindfold, and the fun began. Some bucked, some ran, some stood still until gouged with the spurs, and then they usually did some things.

We broke twenty-five for him that summer, along with our other work. He gave us ten dollars a head.

A sad thing happened to one of our neighbor's little boys that summer. They were an Italian family by the name of Stetter, living on the South side of the river between our place and Belle Fourche. They had two boys, one about sixteen years old, the other two or three. The older boy was mowing alfalfa near the house, and the little fellow was out with him. A neighbor came along and the boy stopped the machine, while they talked for sometime. When the older boy was ready to go on with his mowing, he did not see his small brother, and supposed he had gone to the house, but instead he had gone a short distance ahead of the mower and had gone to sleep in the alfalfa. As the machine came near, he raised himself on his hands, facing the machine, and the older boy, looking back toward the neighbor, did not see the child until the machine struck him, cutting off both hands at the wrists. He stopped the machine before the boy was injured further.

I never heard what became of the child after he grew up, but the older boy always said he would take care of his brother as long as they both lived.

Along toward fall the grass got short, and we moved the cattle up on the head of Dry Creek and herded them where the grass was better. We fenced off a field of a few acres to put them in at night and made a camp. One of us stayed with them all the time. We kept them there until time to turn in on the ranches that fall.

The summer of '89 was another bad mosquito season, and the stock was hard to hold. About July 1, I got a letter from Joe Highshaw saying he had found some of our horses away up on the Little Missouri River in Montana, and had turned them into a man's pasture. He had two in the bunch, and so had others in our neighborhood, so one of us had to go after them. We had one horse that would take lots of riding to break, and it was decided I should go, ride this horse, and tame him. Jone had ridden him a few times, but I had not, and was not sure I could, but we saddled him, I topped him, Jone hazed us out on to the prairie, and we went on our way at a high rate of speed for a few miles, then I pulled him down to a moderate gait. Joe was working for the Three-V that season, and was on the roundup when he found the horses.

I made about fifty miles the first day and stopped with a horseman by the name of Chase on the head of Crow Creek. My horse stood the day's travel fine, and was ready for more the next morning, but was much easier to handle. I went about fifty miles the next day and stopped at a cow-ranch on the Little Missouri River. There was no one at home, but I went in and made myself at home. I found lots of grub, got my supper, and picketed my horse out for the night. Next morning I got my breakfast, saddled up and started on. About the middle of the afternoon I came to the ranch where the horses were, but found no body at home. I went out into the big pasture, found the horses, and ran them into the corral so I could get an early start next morning. This ranch was right on the river and the worst place for mosquitoes I think I ever saw. My horse rolled and fought them all night, and so did I.

As soon as I could see next morning, I started, heading the horses down the river the way I came up, and for the first ten miles, we went some. By that time the horses were hungry enough to stop and grab a mouthful of grass now and then. That made it much easier on my horse. I corralled my horses and stayed at the same place where I had stopped on going up. One of the boys was at home this time. He said they had all been on the roundup.

I did not come back by way of Chase's ranch, but went over the divide on to the head of Owl Creek, then on down the creek, saving considerable distance. I thought I could make it in home by driving late, but it began to rain before night and I saw I could not make it. I knew where a branding corral was on Owl Creek, so I headed my horses for it and got to it just before dark, got them in, fixed up the gate so it would hold them, and tied my horse out on grass for the night. By this time, the rain was coming down about right, but I had my slicker with me and could keep dry. A sensible cowboy ties his slicker on the saddle in the spring and keeps it either there or on his back until fall.

I had eaten nothing since breakfast and was beginning to have a gnawing in my stomach. It rained all night, and I either walked around or leaned up against the corral until morning. As soon as I could see I got those horses out and cut across country for home, getting there by noon with a mighty tired and well-broke horse.

Well, things had been moving in that part of the Territory. The railroad had built on through to the junction of the Redwater and Belle Fourche Rivers, three miles northwest of Minnesela, and had started the town of Belle Fourche. The road missed the town of Minnesela one mile, and consequently, killed it. Seth Bullock, (a cousin of Teddy Roosevelt?) owned more than a section of land at the mouth of Redwater, and gave the railroad enough land for the depot and warehouse. The road crossed the Belle Fourche and built on out two miles on the prairie, where they built stock-pens and got ready to handle the stock which would be shipped from there that fall. All through September and October, the road was very busy, as this was the shipping point for all the country North and West for more than a hundred miles.

Mr. Bullock told the people of Minnesela he would sell them a lot in Belle Fourche for $100.00 and move their buildings to it free of charge. Most of the people moved and Belle Fourche grew very fast. It was a live and wild town for the next few years, especially in the shipping season, when the boys came in to spend their summer wages.

During the summer, the older settlers of our district organized a Sunday School at our school house. A Methodist preacher, who had settled on a claim nearby would come and preach occasionally. My cousin, John Dennison, understood music and was an excellent singer. On Sunday afternoons we would have singing school. You would have been surprised to have seen the crowds we had — cowboys and ranchers would be there for miles around.

The ranchers on the South side of the river formed a company and were building a ditch to irrigate a big scope of country, the ditch to be about fifteen miles long when completed. Water was taken out of Redwater, about two miles South of Minnesela, and the main ditch ran right through the little town. I got the job of doing the plowing on one section of the ditch that fall, and worked until the ground froze.

In August, J. C. Dennison, a brother of John, came out to see the country, and was hired to teach our school the following winter. He made his home with my parents.

The range was getting so settled up we saw we would have to move our cattle farther out, so in October, father took a trip out northeast to look the country over and locate a suitable place. He first went to the Slim Buttes, but found nothing satisfactory. He then pulled across west to the Cave Hills, and stopped to see his old friend, Jack McKenzie, who had the year before settled on Jones Creek, just South of the Cave Hills. They found a good location on up the creek above MacKenzie's place, took a team, hauled up some logs, starting enough improvement on the place to hold it, and then father came back home.

Jones Creek was named for Lame Jones, the noted Buffalo hunter. Our location was where he had his camp while hunting in that country about ten years before.

We had a hot dry spell about the time our wheat, oats, and barley were heading and filling. Seeing that we would not have a full crop, we mowed it and put it up as hay. We needed hay more than grain anyway. The winter of '89-'90 proved to not be a bad one.

In the fall of '89 we sold our first bunch of beef steers. We had also fattened the yoke of cattle brought from Nebraska, and let them go with the beef steers to Zoekles Bros., butchers in Deadwood.

It was in '89 that the territory was divided and South Dakota was admitted to the Union. I recall that one of our neighbors came over to our place when he first heard we were in a state and said he would have to move on, as he never had and never would live in a state—the place was getting too tame for him.

I was making arrangements to prove up on my homestead in the spring, so that I would be able to go out with the cattle. While we were waiting for the grass to start, we put out some small grain and did some plowing, as father said he would keep one team and cultivate the crop in the valley. About that time cousin J. C. bought a few cattle and put them in with ours, as he was going to help us on our cow-ranch the coming summer.

Except for a few snows through April, it was quite dry and grass was slow in starting, but by May 15, we had everything together and started with the cattle. Our sister was going to drive the wagon and we boys the cattle. We knew we would have to go slowly, as some of the cows were thin, and there would be calves coming. We had our tent, beds, and camp outfit, and by the time we got it all in, it made a heavy load, as the ground was soft. There wasn't any road—just a trail across the prairie—but we had a good team and sister could drive a team as well as the best. We had a good canvas on the wagon and could close up the ends to keep warm, because it always got cold of nights. Sister slept in the wagon and we boys in the tent.

We stood guard, the first three nights, but the cattle were so quiet and contented that we did not bother after that. The cattle would begin to move at daylight, and two of us would round them up and keep them headed in the right direction while the other took care of the team, helped get, and eat his breakfast, then came on and managed the herd while the other two ate breakfast and broke camp. We kept that up for eleven days. A good many animals had to be pulled out of the muddy creeks, and sometimes we would have two or three calves in the hind-end of the wagon, but we had good weather all the way through.

When we got to our destination, we took a day to look the land over, then decided to put our buildings at the mouth of a canyon that came out of the mountain on the South side, where we would be sheltered from the northwest and east storms; and a nice stream of water coming down out of the mountain—an ideal place for the ranch improvements. So we drove up there next day, pitched camp, set up the big tent, fitted out our cook stove under a tree, finding plenty of timber for wood nearby, put everything else in the tent, and went to bed that night feeling fine.

But the next morning there was a cold drizzling rain, the wind was rising, and the cattle were beginning to drift with the storm. It kept one of us with them all day, and that night we took turns on guard. It rained all night and all next day, but we had good slickers and stood it very well.

The next day it cleared, we went to cutting poles for a corral, and got warm again. In a couple of days we had up a good one. After a week's work, sister and I started home, leaving the boys to run things. They had supplies to run them until July, when I planned to go out and help them put up hay. It was about one hundred miles from the cow-ranch home and there was just one house in sight on the road between the two places—that was Macy's postoffice, just half-way. We made the trip home in two days.

It might be well to give you a short description of "Cave Hill" at this time. It is about twelve miles square and looks like that much earth pushed up out of the prairie, is perfectly flat on top, and around the rim is from twenty-five to one hundred feet straight up and down. There are only a few places on the south side where one can get a horse up or down, and only one place allows a team. The canyons, running back into the hill, have steep sides of the same order. This mesa made the north line of our pasture fence, which we erected in the fall of '90. We had only two small gaps to fence in order to make a good four-mile boundary. Our posts were obtained from the timber in the canyons and were mostly pine and ash.

When we moved out, there were eight ranchers, all small cow-men, in the hills. It certainly was a good location for cattle and horses, as water and grass were in abundance.

I stayed on my claim in the valley until July, then proved up, got my patent, and after harvest was over, bought a new mowing machine, rake, and other tools for the coming hay season. I got a supply of grub, rigged up some more harness, and about July 15, hitched four horses to the wagon, led two, and pulled out for the cow-ranch. We needed three teams in haying. It took me three days to make the trip out.

When I got to the ranch, the boys were getting ready to go to a prairie fire which had been raging over on Bull Creek, six miles away. We got over just after dark, and found all the settlers in the hills there, hard at it. We would build back-fires against the main fire and whip them out with slickers and wet sacks before they got too much of a start, making a burned strip too wide for the main fire to cross. We worked until daylight before we got it under control.

On the way home that morning we saw another fire down southwest, and after we got some breakfast, Jone and I started out to see how far this one was from our ranch. J. C. stayed at the ranch, as he was not feeling well. We found the fire about six miles away, and headed in the direction of the ranch. As the wind was not bad, we began to whip it out and made pretty good headway as long as the ground was rough, but when it would strike a smooth place with big grass, it would get so hot we could do nothing with it. The day was very hot and we suffered terribly with thirst, as there was nothing but alkali water, and we knew better than to drink that. About three in the afternoon, a whirl-wind came along and carried the fire as fast as a horse could run. We were so nearly played out, that was enough for us, so we got our horses and went to camp to wait until night, hoping the wind would die out.

When we got in, J. C. was feeling somewhat better, although he had not eaten a thing all day. He said he would go over the mountain and let the fellows know, as we were sure they knew nothing of the later fire.

We got a bite to eat, then fell over asleep, not waking until J. C. got back after dark. He brought all the Bull Creek fellows with him, and we saddled up and struck out for the fire. J. C. went along, saying he could hold the horses, if not able to fight fire.

The wind had gone down but the fire looked big and close. We soon got to it, and went after it with a vengeance, as it was getting too close home for comfort. There was a little cloud in the west which looked as though we might get a sprinkle. About midnight we had it under control and were waiting for a little strip to burn out between two small creeks. I told the boys I would go back and look about an area in some badlands which had flared up a little. J. C. kept my horse. I found the fire on a flat between two "draws," where it could not get out, and started back to the rest of the gang, when it began to sprinkle, and in ten minutes there wasn't a spark to be seen.

I kept along the edge of the burn, thinking I would find the boys soon. I walked and walked, finding no one, and after I had walked myself down, I sat down to wait for daylight and went to sleep. When I awoke it was daytime and I did not know where I was—it was all new country to me. I went over and climbed a small butte nearby and from there I could see the hills, but I was northwest instead of southwest of them. While I was on the butte, I saw a man on horseback about two miles south of me. He saw me and we started toward each other. I found him to be one of our neighbors who had started to the fire, and when the sprinkle came, leaving all in darkness, he had sense enough to unsaddle his horse and lie down until daylight.

The boys had gone a little way from the edge of the burn and waited for me until morning. I had walked more than twelve miles over a rough country. We all got to camp about the same time, had breakfast, and I got acquainted with the Cave Hill neighbors. It was a good thing we got the fire put out the night before, for the wind blew a gale from the southwest all that day, and it certainly would have cleaned us out.

We put our machinery together, made hay-frames, and were ready to make hay in a few days. The hay was good and close at hand, so with the three teams and two wagons, we got along rapidly. The cattle were putting on fat with grass and water so plentiful, and they took very little tending.

The boys had cut several hundred posts and had dug almost all the postholes for the west line of our fence, in all about three miles long, leading across the Jones Creek valley. The mountain south of Jones Creek was not as high or as rough as the one on the north, where our buildings were to be, so we had to fence several gaps on that side. The east boundary joined one neighbor, McKenzie, and he put up half of that fence. In all we built about five miles of line, enclosing between eight and ten thousand acres of about as fine grass as anyone ever saw. The canyons running back into north mountain were very rough, so our stock could get shelter from any direction of wind, with plenty of springs for water which scarcely ever froze.

We put up hay for nearly two months and were sure we had enough to take us through the winter, as we did not plan on feeding anything except the calves and thin cows. I had brought what wire I could up with the machinery, with which we fenced the hay. This done, J. C. and I pulled for the Belle Fourche Valley. He was going to teach our school again that winter.

When we got home, we found some more of our relatives from W. Va., Gene Dunnington, his wife, and child. Gene was a railroad man. His health had failed, and he was advised to go to a high dry climate. Gene and I cut the corn, got up our wood for the winter, and got ready to go back to the ranch, to be there in time to help ship the beef. I had to take a supply of grub to run until spring, for I wanted no more travelling with a wagon in winter time. I also took a supply of wire, and made another three day trip back to the Cave Hills, loaded heavily.

When I got out to the ranch, the arrangements were all made to start the beef in about four days, so we rushed around to get ready. Jone had the posts all hauled and had dug a hole back in the mountain to make a dugout to live in during the winter. We cut a log for the ridge pole and hauled rock to wall up the front so I could be working on it while he was gone with the beef.

All of us, "Hill-Billies," as we were called, threw our beef together and drove them to the railroad, making a train-load. It was one hundred miles to Dickinson and the Northern Pacific, the same distance as the Belle Fourche, and as the grass was better to the north, we decided to go that way. Each outfit was to get its cattle to a certain place on the 11th, and would start the next day with the herd. Jone and I gathered ours, cut out the beef, and got to the starting point on time. All the other boys came in with theirs, and we had a regular outfit, just like a round-up cook wagon, bed-wagon, horse-wrangler, and cook. The first night was always the hardest, and it took most of us to hold them together, there being so many different herds and all wanting to go back home. We always elected a foreman for the drive, and Alex Connell had the job on this trip.

I stayed with the boys the first night, then went back home. Jone went to the railroad and came back with the cook-wagon, leaving our two loads of steers in the care of Connell. It took ten days to get to Dickinson and two to come back. I had most of the posts set when Jone got back. Then we went to work on the dugout.

It faced south, and measured 14 by 16 feet, was walled in front with rock, had a door in the center, a window on each side, and a heavy log on top of the wall. A log was then put on each side, with one big log in the middle for a ridge pole. Then we laid nice straight poles close together with some hay on top to keep the dirt from coming through, and covered the whole thing with more than a foot of dirt. We then moved in, put in a cook-stove, built a cupboard close to the stove, made two bunks in the back part, then made a table fastened to two posts in the side of the wall, and put hinges on it so we could let it down when not in use. Next came several chairs out of dry-goods boxes, then we wet the gumbo floor and pounded it until it was as hard as a rock, and we were ready for housekeeping.

We finished our fence, rounded up all our cattle, and got them into the pasture by Nov. 12. We had no stable for our team and saddle horses yet, but with plenty of timber close by, it did not take long to put up one that was good and warm, built out of logs, chinked with gumbo, covered with poles and hay—not waterproof, to be sure, but that did not worry us in winter time and we did not need it in summer.

Jone had told Connell to have the proceeds from the cattle sent to father at Belle Fourche, as we were doing business under the name of A. J. Hamilton & Sons. We did not have any word from home, so did not yet know how much they weighed. Connell said they sold for $4.00 per hundred, and we were guessing them at 1200 lbs. each. The rest of the shipment did not run over $3.50 per hundred. Ours were a fine bunch of Shorthorn and Hereford grade steers.

About Nov. 25 we got a big snow a foot deep on the level, and as there was no wind, and it was not very cold, it did not blow off the high places. The cattle could get nothing to eat, and we knew if we began feeding hay that early, the cattle would not rustle, making feeding necessary the rest of the winter. We had brought a couple of 2 by 12 timbers 14 feet long for just such an emergency. These we bolted together at one end and spread them about seven apart at the other, spiked a 2 by 6 across the top to hold them in place, hitched the heaviest team on we had, and pulled out. The cattle fell right in behind us as though we were unloading hay. We fed them that way for about ten days before the snow got off enough for them to graze again.

One day after we got through with the snow-plowing, Jone said he thought he would go over the mountain and get some meat, as our supply was running low. So he took his Winchester and pulled up over the hill. I sat around for awhile, and then thought I would try my hand at baking a pie, so I got things together, having my apricots already cooked, made the dough nice and thin, put the bottom crust in, poured in the fruit, and put on the top crust. I had put in plenty of apricots, for I always did like plenty of insides to a pie, and I was pleased with the looks of it. I then shoved her in the stove and sat down to read a dime novel. When I thought it should be about done, I opened the stove door, and lo and behold! the oven was full of pie. I took it out and at first thought I would throw it away where Jone would not see it. But it smelled so good I changed my mind, no difference if he did laugh at me. I went on and got dinner for I knew I could fry meat, bake biscuits, and make coffee.

So I had it all ready (I had the pie covered up) when he came in, and he said, "I'm glad you have dinner ready, for I'm as hungry as a wolf."

I asked, "Have any luck?"

"Yes, I killed the biggest black-tail buck I ever saw, and it is just up the mountain, not more than half a mile away."

It was three miles to where we could get up on top with a wagon, so we decided to take a rope, tie the buck's legs together, swing it on a pole, and carry it.

That decided, we sat down to dinner. After we finished the main course, I brought out the pie.

After he looked at it awhile, he said, "Say, what do you call that?"

"An apricot pie," I answered.

Then he fell over. After he got so he could talk a little, he demanded: "Tell me just how you mixed that dough."

"Why just like I mix biscuit dough, of course."

And then he had another spell. After awhile he said, "One thing good about it, we have enough pie to last all winter, anyway—just like you when you cooked the first rice." So that is how I got out of cooking from then on when we were batching.

After dinner we took a rope and a pole and went for the deer. Jone took his gun, and when we got about to the place, out jumped three yearling does. Jone got one, then followed around the point and got the other two. So now the team became a necessity. We dressed the three and hung them up in a tree where the wolves could not get them. But the buck was so big we could not hang him up high enough. So we swung him on the pole and started home. I think he weighed about 175 pounds when we started, but I know he weighed 400 by the time we got him home through that snow. The next day, after we fed the cattle, we went out to the west end of the mountain, where we could get up with the team, got the three others, and had venison until we got tired of it.

About Dec. 1, McKenzie came over from his ranch and brought us a letter from home that had been written about

Nov. 1, stating that the steers had weighed a little over 1250 pounds. We were well pleased. That was the first shipment we had made, for what cattle we had sold before moving out north had gone to local butchers in the hills.

Our big snow went off and we had fine weather up until Christmas. The cattle were doing fine. We were feeding nothing but the calves we had weaned in the fall, keeping them in the corral.

With things so quiet, we had some time to visit with our neighbors. McKenzie was our nearest. His ranch house was about five miles from us. George Dell was the next nearest—he lived six miles away, over on Bull Creek.

So that a better idea may be gotten of the Cave Hills, I will describe them a little more fully. The Hills are divided into three parts by Jones and Bull Creeks. The hills south of Jones Creek are less rough than those on the north. South Grand River is still farther south of the Hills. Bull Creek runs east, dividing the hills and making the roughest part lie between Jones and Bull Creeks. Still north of this section is North Grand River, about four miles north of the line between North and South Dakota. McKenzie and ourselves were the only ones living on Jones Creek. George Dell, Joe Johnson, his nephew, Gene, and Alex Connell, all lived on Bull Creek. Pierce Black and Ed McCumsey had a ranch on the east side, about five miles north of Connell's on Spring Creek. The Curless family of father and three sons were on the north side by a big spring on the head of Crooked Creek. Charley Vansickle was west of the Hills at the foot of Table Mountain, a high flat-topped hill with no timber except ash in the canyons running back in the hill.

I neglected to say that when we got the letter from father in regard to the beef, I also got two letters that were of great importance. They were from that West Virginia girl of mine. The last one written roasted me considerably for not answering the first, so I had to explain that I was 50 miles from the post office and could write only when some of the neighbors went that way. But I got to send one out pretty soon, as our neighbor McKenzie went down to his home ranch for Christmas. In this I assured her I would always have one written and send it out the first chance.

While we were busy on the ranch, big things were going on down in Butte County. Belle Fourche was booming, and lots of people were moving away from Minnesela. Seth Bullock built a good big square building in Belle Fourche and said that if the people of the county would vote the county seat there at the election in the fall, he would donate this building for a courthouse. As they had no court house in Minnesela, and were renting a small building for the purpose, it carried by a big majority and everybody was happy—or almost everybody.

We kept very comfortable and did not have to chop much wood—just enough to cook with, and that kept us warm. We had venison all winter, and did not kill a beef.

The Indians scared the game pretty badly that fall. Old Sitting Bull and some of his tribe had been in the Hills— thirteen wagons of them—and they killed a good many animals, but not as many as the same number of white men would have, for Indians are very poor marksmen. But they go in such droves and shoot so much they scare everything out of the country.

That was the only time I ever saw Sitting Bull. He was not more than 5 feet 7 inches tall, but the broadest man across the shoulders I ever saw—not very deep through the chest, and probably not weighing more than 175 or 180 pounds. That was his last trip to the Hills, as he was killed less than a month later. I will have more to say about him and the rest of the Sioux tribe later.

I got well acquainted with our neighbors that winter, and they were a fine bunch of fellows. Almost everyone in the range country has a nickname—lots of them after the part of the country from which they came. In many cases, I never knew anything but the nicknames. I knew three fellows going by the name of "Missouri," one being "Big Missouri," one "Little Missouri," and my cousin, Will Hamilton, just plain "Missouri." I am sure there were lots of cowboys who knew no name for me but "Virginia." If I should go back there now and meet any of the boys, they would be sure to greet me by my old moniker.

About Dec. 1, 1890, we began hearing about the Indians getting restless down on the reservation. Sitting Bull, their noted chief, was trying to incite the Sioux tribe to war. They were having their war dances, and Sitting Bull and his medicine-men were telling them there would be a very mild winter, so they could pull up through the northern part of South Dakota and join the Crows in Montana, giving them enough strength to drive the whites out of the northwest.

Jack McKenzie was up to our ranch one Sunday and we were talking over what we had heard about the disturbance. We got just enough news to make us uneasy. After the big snow went off, Jone had gone down to the settlement to spend the holidays and I was alone. Jack had been caught in the Big Horn Mountains with a bunch of mining men and trappers in '76, the year Custer was killed, so he was wise to their ways. He said thirty-six of them went in together and the soldiers came in to escort them out. There were only eighteen left when they got out. The Indians had the rest. He said if a man tells you he is not afraid of Indians, he is either a fool, or knows nothing about them.

Just after I went to bed that night, I heard someone call, and I went to the door. It was Jack. He said Sitting Bull had been killed and the Sioux had left the Reservation, heading for our part of the country, killing and plundering as they went. Joe Driskill, foreman of the E6 Ranch, and Bill Bankston, an E6 hand, were with him. We were not in shape to take much of a defence as most of the boys had gone down to the settlement for the holidays. One of the E6 boys was up on Bull Creek that day and saw two scouts who said there was a company of soldiers stationed at Camp Crook, about thirty-five miles southwest of the Hills. The scouts said it would be better for all the boys from the Cave Hills to go there.

Joe sent the boy who had seen the scouts on to Spearfish, in the Black Hills, where the state was giving out guns to the settlers, to get some guns, and all the boys he could get together; then to get back as soon as possible. All who were in the Cave Hills were to gather at the George Dell ranch on Bull Creek.

So I turned out all the stock I had in the shed, not knowing when I would be back, saddled my horse, got my rifle, and we started. It was about six miles across the mountains, and was very dark. When we got to Dell's we found no one, and the stock turned out. Joe Johnson's ranch was about three miles on down the creek. Thinking they might have changed their minds after sending out their messenger and had decided on the Johnson Ranch, we went on over there.

When we went in the Johnson house, we found nobody there, but the way things were torn up, it was plain to see they had left in a hurry. The supper was all on the table, chairs turned over, bedclothes strewed around, and everything topsy-turvy. There was no stock in the barn, and we had no idea where everybody was.

Alex Connell's ranch was on down the creek about four miles, and that was our next stop. Here again we found an empty, though this time an orderly house. Connell's stallion was not in the barn.

It was evident that the boys had gotten a scare at Johnson's and had pulled out for Camp Crook. We were pretty sore lot to think the way they had treated us, but we decided we had done enough riding that night, so Joe and I stood first guard and Jack and Bill went in the house to catch a few winks. It was after midnight by that time.

We had not been on guard an hour until Jack came out to us and asked if we had called him. I said not. He said, "I heard my name called twice, as plain as I ever heard it, and if you boys did not call me, I am going away from this place. You may call me superstitious if you like, but I think this is a good place to be away from." And as he was much the older one of us, we thought he should be boss. It was about five miles across to Jack's place, so he said we would go there and stay until morning.

His house was of logs and stood out in the open, so no one could approach it without being in plain sight. We went to bed and slept until daylight. After breakfast we talked a while and were in a quandary as to what to do. It was evident that we were the only men in the Cave Hills. We had no evidence that there were Indians near us. It would be at least three days before the messenger could get back with the guns and reenforcements. Jack and I had Winchester rifles, while Joe and Bill had only their six-guns.

We finally decided to go down to the E6 ranch, fifteen miles down the creek. We thought one of the boys might get back and have some news. As we went down, we kept near the creek, riding up on high ground now and then to search the country with glasses Jack hid with him, but saw nothing but cattle and horses.

We stayed at the E6 that night and until evening the next day, then after leaving a note for the boys, we went back to Jack's place, and the next day on to our ranch. The following day Jone got in and said quite a bunch of the boys had gone on to the ranches with guns and ammunition. He had an army gun apiece for us, and he gave us some news. He said there had been big excitement down in the hills. The ranchers had all gathered in the towns when the news came Sitting Bull had been killed and the Indians had started to leave their reservation. Minnesela and Belle Fourche both threw up breastworks and fortified themselves, with picket duty, for a week. They got word that every rancher in the Cave Hills had been killed. When they heard this, quite a bunch started out to us, but when they got to Macy, they found it was a mistake. Some of them went back. Jone came on with the others until within ten miles of home, then cut across and came on home alone.

In a few days after Jone came, a company of soldiers were stationed at the E6 ranch, and one was sent to Camp

Crook before the battle of Wounded Knee, and were kept there until late in the winter.

The battle of Wounded Knee took place on December 29. Sitting Bull had been killed about two weeks before that, when a small bunch of Sioux scouts were sent out to arrest and bring him to the Agency. He resisted arrest, was shot and killed, and all but one of the scouts were killed.

With the Sioux decisively beaten at Wounded Knee, things soon settled back to normal again, and Jone, McKenzie, and I went over to the Dell Ranch one Sunday to find out what scared them out of the country, and it sure was amusing to hear them tell it.

After they had sent word to Jack and me, they had decided they would be better off at the Johnson ranch, so they all went there, and while getting supper, they put two of boys on guard. There was a good many big rocks against the hill above the ranch-house. It was night time, but not so dark but that they could see objects moving about among the rocks. So those boys, seeing some cows grazing, ran to the house and reported they saw Indians slipping up on them from the rear. They all jumped up from the table, got their horses, some bedding for saddle blankets, and pulled for Camp Crook, every fellow for himself and the devil for the hindmost. The many funny things that happened on that forty-mile trip would fill a small book.

The winter was the mildest I ever saw, after the snow we had early in the season. I wanted to go down to the Hills to see what was going on after the scare was over, so in January I started out, one rather cold windy morning. Going horseback, we always went straight south after getting out of our south gate, and came into the old Dickinson freight road at Grand River.

Just as I came out of a gulch at the river's edge, I saw two Indians coming on horseback toward me at top speed. I knew they were Indians by the flapping of their blankets, and I whirled my horse back into the canyon to a high bluff where they could get to only one side, so they would have to face me. I was ready for them the moment they would round the bend. As soon as they came in sight I saw they were scouts, and when they came up. they were very much amused at me for being scared. They were Indian scouts on their way from the E6 to Camp Crook, and wanted to ask me the direction.

When I got home, mother had a letter from my Uncle Jim Hamilton stating he had seen in the Kingwood (W. Va.) Journal where father and we boys had all been killed by the Indians. Afterward, a cousin sent us the clipping. It told of a Preston County, W. Va., man and his two sons being killed and scalped by the Indians on their cow-ranch in South Dakota. The story went on to tell how they had been surrounded while herding their cattle, and how valiantly they had fought to their deaths rather than be captured and tortured. The editor of the Journal was a particular friend of my father, and father wrote to him to find out how he got such a story. He answered that he had copied it from another newspaper.

I did not stay in the settlement long, as I was afraid it would storm and make bad travelling. Everything was quiet when I got back to the cow-ranch.

It was a little trying that winter, living in the dugout. We would often have five or six of the boys in and they would smoke until the air was blue. Neither of us smoked, so when the air got too thick, I would make some excuse to get outside for awhile.

The Cave Hills got their name from the fact that there is a cave of considerable extent in the northeast side of one of the group. I have been in as far as one hundred and fifty yards, and it has been explored much farther than that. The entrance is not large—about the size of an ordinary door—but as one goes farther back, the passage gets much larger. There are narrow places, so that a man can scarcely get through, then it will open up into a space the size of a large room. I don't know the distance it has been explored.

In passing, I should say something about the fruits of

our hills. We had the most wonderful wild plums I ever saw. They grew in all the canyons, and along all the creeks of the prairie. Some are just like the Wild Goose which grows in nearly all parts of the U. S. Some were fully as large as the Wild Goose, but were golden in color, and some were small and red, called hog-plums, good for jelly only. We also had the June-berry, growing in the gulches of the hills. They tasted and looked considerably like our Virginia Service Berry, but were much larger. The Indians gathered and dried them for winter use. The Buffalo Berry grew along the creeks and were very sour and red, somewhat smaller than a currant, and very fine for jelly. The Choke Cherry was much like the common wild cherry. All these fruits grew on small bushes, seldom getting larger than a man's wrist. The sand cherry was a fine fruit, tasting something like the old Sweetheart cherry of Virginia. Wild gooseberries and currants grew in profusion in the canyons.

Well, spring had warmed up, grass was getting pretty good, and we had to have some supplies, so, as I was always considered the farmer of the family, and we wanted to put out a pretty good lot of corn, it was time for me to go down to the settlement. I think it was about April 20 that I started. I took a team, and with no load, made it to Macy the first day. Effie Oliver, a step-daughter of Mr. Macy, wanted to go down with me to visit sister and mother for awhile. As our team would be coming back in about ten days, she got ready and we started about seven.

It looked a little like rain, but we had a cover on the wagon, so we thought we could keep dry, anyway. We made good time until about midafternoon, when it began to drizzle. We were then about eight miles north of Indian Creek. The summer before, several settlers had come in on Indian Creek. Mel Fasberry had married one of our neighbor's girls, and they had a ranch right where we crossed the creek. I told Effie not to be uneasy, that we would surely make it to the Fasberry's. It did not rain hard, but we had not gone far until the gumbo began to roll up. It was mostly downgrade, but the mud would roll up until it began to rub against the sides of the wagon bed, and when all four wheels got to rubbing, the team couldn't pull it, even if it was downhill.

I always carried a spade with me, so I would get out and punch mud off, and it was no small job when the wheels, spokes, and all were solid with mud. We would go but a few rods until every wheel would be full again. We kept that up until both the team and myself were pretty nearly all in. Finally I said the team would have to rest a while, so we ate what lunch we had left, and then I gave the wheels a good punching. It had quit raining, but was so dark I could not see ahead of the team. I was sure we were not more than two or three miles from the Fasberry place. It got so dark I could not keep the team in the road, so I got out and cleaned the gumbo off and told Effie I would lead awhile, for I was afraid if we got away from the road, I would never find it again. As we got nearer the creek, the mud was not so bad and we made better time. Finally something loomed up in front of me, I stopped the team and went to see what it was, and to my great joy, it was Fasberry's hay-rick I went on to his house, called him out with a lantern, got the team unhooked, and the girl to the house, and our troubles were over. It was then about ten at night. If I had been alone, I would have camped when night came on.

The next morning we went on home, with the gumbo rolling in only a few places. I found the folks all well and glad to hear that everything had gone well with us through the winter. Gene Dunnington had gone to work for Cap Knight over on False-bottom. Gene was working the farm and his wife was doing the cooking, as Knight kept two or three hands. J. C. Dennison's school was out. John Dennison was working for McMaster, and Clarkson was still with the same man, Hank Stearns. J. C. wanted to go out to the ranch again, for the summer, so we began getting his load together. I went to a sawmill up near Deadwood after some lumber, and we sent for flour, bacon, potatoes, and groceries. Mother added a dozen hens, and J. C. and Effie pulled out about May 1. They went as far as Fasberry's the first evening, made it to Macy next day, and J. C. got to the ranch late the next night. Jone planted some potatoes so we could have our own supply.

The spring stayed fine, so we got out a pretty good crop of corn. We did not sow any small grain.

We had no Sunday School during the winter, but the first of May, we organized one with father as superintendent. We had singing almost every Sunday afternoon and preaching once a month by a man named Glidden. We had a good attendance, for it was a common place for all the settlers to meet and visit, and as it was somewhat a novelty, most of them took an active part.

The mosquitoes were pretty bad that June and a small bunch of our horses left us. We were short on saddle horses at the home ranch, having most all the rideable ones at the cow-ranch. A neighbor boy got a job riding line for the Three-V for the summer, and had as pretty a little snow-white Arabian horse as I ever saw—and as quick as a cat. The boy, Pete Nelson, had worked a trick on Frank Brian, a horseman, to get him. Pete was breaking horses to ride and Frank told him he wanted this young horse "broke good and gentle" for himself, as he was a poor rider. Pete tried to buy him, could not, so decided to spoil him and buy him afterwards at his own price. After he was pretty well broken in, he taught him to buck. Frank was afraid of him and soon sold him to Pete for $30.00.

Pete said he would like me to take this horse and ride him through the summer, for if he turned him out, he might not find him when he came back from work in the fall. I, being short of horses, was glad to get him, and, like Pete, I wanted him and tried to buy him but could not. I knew Pete was as good a rider as I, but he was very slow in getting mounted, and I never saw the horse I could not get on after I got him by the head and had my right hand on the saddle horn.

So I thought to myself, "if I can spoil him in getting

on so he will start too quick for Pete and land him behind the saddle, he'll throw him, and then he might sell him to me." And I began trying. I would start him and mount as he was going, and he was a very apt pupil. It was not a week until he was gone as soon as my foot struck the stirrup, and a fellow had to know his business if he didn't land behind the saddle. If he did, Whitie had not forgotten his old trick, and he would buck the rider off every time.

A young man by the name of Crawford came out that spring from W. Va. to see us. Mother and sister had never been out to the ranch, and they, with two sisters by the name of Bird, who had settled on a claim near us, all wanted to see the north country. So when the June berries were ripe, they got things together and started about mid-June.

The Bird girls went in a one horse buggy, and father, mother, sister, and Crawford in the roadwagon took some supplies to the boys to last until I would go out to make hay. They made the trip out in two days and had a fine time exploring the hills and gathering berries. Crawford was so pleased with the country he said he would like to stay with us the coming winter. They were gone ten days. Coming back, the girls' horse got loose when they camped near Macy and came on home. So they all came home in the wagon with the buggy tied on behind.

After they got home, I thought I had better take a look for the horses the mosquitoes had chased out of the country. I was certain they had gone northwest, as the wind had come from that direction most of the summer. I rode the white horse, as I knew it would be a hard ride and he was the one to get to the end of the road in a hurry. I went by Belle Fourche and on up Crow Creek to my old friend Chase's ranch and stopped with him for the night. I was sure that if the horses were anywhere in that part of the country, he would know it, as his horses ranged up there and he was riding after them every day. He stayed there only during the summer, and had only summer shelter. He was away when I reached the ranch but came in before nightfall.

Chase had a very queer pet—a pig, weighing about 150 lbs. He had no pen for him, and he appeared to be a priviledged character, as he went wherever he pleased and did pretty much as he wished. Chase did his cooking out in the yard, and it kept him pretty busy keeping the pig out of the potatoes while they were frying.

He told me he had seen my horses a couple of days before over near Pete Nelson's line camp, and as he wanted to ride that way, he would go with me next day.

When it came bedtime, he gave me a couple of blankets and with my saddle blankets, and my saddle for a pillow, I had a very good bed on the floor. It was warm, so we left the door open to get what air we could. I was tired and went to sleep as soon as I shut my eyes.

But something wakened me in the night, and I heard heavy breathing near me. Putting out my hand to investigate, I contacted Mr. Hog, snoozing comfortably on the edge of my bed. As he was a fat fellow and snoring so I couldn't go to sleep again, I decided to put him out and shut the door; but that was easier said than done, for it was dark in the house and he elected to stay inside. I didn't know the location of things in the house as well as the hog did, so I had to call on Chase to light a lamp, to give me an idea of the lay of the land. After I could see, and got some assistance from Chase, I succeeded in getting "His Hog ship" out and the door shut. After that we were disturbed no more.

We went over to the line camp next morning, looking at all the horses we saw, but did not run on to mine. Pete was on line when we got there, so we began stirring up some dinner, and just as we had it ready, he came. He was glad to see me, as he had not been down in the settlement since he left in the spring. He said he had seen the horses I was after the day before about five miles out on the divide, and that they had been in that locality for several days. So after we had visited awhile, he said he would go out with me. Chase went on back to his ranch.

As we started, Pete said: "I see you have Whitie in good flesh. You have not ridden him much."

"No," I said, "I have not used him very much, as I have no cattle to look after—just the horses to run in once in a while."

"You better ride him more or he will get at his old tricks again and if he does I say he is hard to ride."

"Whitie and I understand each other pretty well," I answered.

We found the horses about the middle of the afternoon. Pete had no place to corral them over night, so I thought I would start them and run them to the roundup corral on Owl Creek. He helped me to get them started. I knew it to be only about fifteen or sixteen miles down the creek to the corral, and I could make it by dark. They drove fine, and about sundown we were at the corral. As I was alone, I knew I would have some trouble getting them in, and I sure had a hot horse when it was finished. I fastened the bars good and tight then led my horse down to the creek for water, as neither of us had had a drink since we left the line camp.

By this time, the mosquitoes were getting fierce. I knew if we stayed in the bottom, neither would get any rest, so I rode out on the divide where the wind was blowing some, unsaddled Whitie, picketed him on good grass, and rolled up in my saddle blankets for the night. The coyotes must have been having a camp meeting that night, for I never heard them make so much noise.

Next morning I started early, and was home by noon.

John Dennison was still working for McMaster, and Crawford got a job there also, working until fall. It was time now to begin putting up hay. I had to take some repairs for the machine, and grub to run until fall. Isaac Arpan, a boy who lived on Indian Creek, was going out with me to look after the cattle while we put up hay. It was now about the middle of July.

I loaded up and drove to Indian Creek, so Isaac could get ready to go with me next morning. I took Whitie with me, for father said he would not ride him, and didn't want to be bothered with him. Ike and I pulled out next day and made it to the ranch in two days.

We found the boys well but low on grub. They said they had lived mostly on eggs for two or three days past. Jone had killed a deer the day we got there, and they had some nice young chickens. But they said they did not like to live on meat alone.

We got everything rigged up and went to cutting hay. It was good, but we had to go some distance to get it, as we didn't want to cut inside the pasture, and the cattle ranged close outside. It was about five miles from our west fence to the top of the divide between Jones Creek and the Little Missouri River, and there was no lasting water more than a mile west of the fence. So the cattle had to come back near home to water, making them easy to hold, but made us go farther for the hay. They scarcely ever got to the top of the divide—only in the spring when it was raining a lot. Then we had to ride line to keep them from going over the divide. We would make a circle of about fifteen miles, throwing all cattle back toward the ranch. In that way, scarcely any got away.

The worst trouble was in keeping the range cattle from coming in. If they got to bothering too badly, some very still mornings we would go out on the divide and shoot a few times, give three or four keen yells, and we would see those old wild steers come out of the badlands on the run, and they would run clear over into Montana and not get back for a month. But if any of our yearlings happened to be with them, it was just too bad, for they would out-run the whole bunch.

Isaac got used to the cattle and the range and did fine work. The haying was going splendidly. It was very dry, so we were keeping a lookout for prairie fires. There was one raging over back of Table Mountain about fifteen miles away, but we didn't go to it. Jone went with the roundup for awhile when it passed our way and got a few yearling over on the Little Missouri.

When it was too windy to handle hay, we cut and hewed logs for a house, and by fall had almost enough to build a house 16 by 24 feet, one story high. We had also built some more shelter sheds.

As J. C. had hired to teach the Ingersoll school, he had to be going in, so he took a team and went down about the middle of September. About Oct. 1, we shipped the beef. Jone went to Chicago with them, and while he was away, Ike and I turned the cattle in the pasture, as water was getting scarce outside. When Jone got back, we went down to bring out our bunch of horses.

The next day, Pete came home from the line camp and took Whitie on down home with him. He lived about half a mile southeast of us. I looked down that way that evening and saw Whitie running with the saddle on him. I called Jone and pointed that way, and directly I saw Pete out a-foot, driving Whitie toward the barn. After a while, I saw him coming across the prairie on his other horse and leading Whitie. He came on to the house, and as we went out to meet him I asked "What's the matter?"

He said "You know what's the matter. This infernal horse has thrown me twice this evening."

I said "You're a better rider than I and he never threw me."

"Yes, but I can't get on him," said Pete.

I said, "I'll show you how to get on a horse." And I got my saddle and put it on him, patted him on the neck, then slipped my hand down, catching the cheek-piece of the bridle, at the same time grabbing the horn of the saddle, and was in the saddle before he got one jump.

Pete said, "Yes, but you know I can't do that. I always light behind the saddle."

Jone spoke up and asked, "What will you take for him, Pete?"

"I want thirty dollars, just what I paid for him."

Jone paid him, and don't you know, he would never let me have that horse!

We got our horses all rounded up and ready so we could get an early start next morning, for it was a fifty mile drive to Macy, and that was the only place we could corral them until we got to the ranch. We got started real early, and, of course, Jone would ride the white horse. I was in hopes he would land behind the saddle, but no such luck. We stopped and let the horses graze for an hour just after we got over Two-top divide, about twenty five miles out, then reached Macy with time left to graze them awhile before corraling them for the night. We got a good start next morning and got inside the pasture before dark, with a pair of very tired horses, for it is hard to drive a bunch of horses through a strange country.

We had taken the yearling, two-year old, and three-year old fillies out in the spring, and had gotten a young Percheron horse to turn with them. The next day we gathered them, turned them all together in the pasture, and kept them all in that winter, for I knew the old mares would go back home if they were turned loose.

We found everything all right, as the cattle were all inside the fence. We had heard of a man down in the Belle Fourche valley who had come from Missouri with some good Hereford cattle, and we wanted to improve our herd as fast as possible, so, after talking to some of our neighbors, Joe and Gene Johnson, who wanted to improve their stock also, it was arranged for Joe to go in with us. We planned to go down and see the Herefords, and on the way back, bring some cattle and another team from home. So we all went down horseback and left Isaac to take care of the ranch.

Crawford had quit at McMaster's, and he and father

had up a nice lot of wood. As we were taking everything back to the ranch but two or three cows, one team, and the stallion, father would not have much to look after.

We had shipped two loads of dry cows and steers, getting $4.25 for the steers, weighing about 1225 lbs. apiece, the cows weighed about 1100 and brought $2.75. This was not quite as much as in the fall before, but we were well satisfied.

Jone and Joe went to see the Hereford cattle and were gone about four days. The owner, McPherson, was a widower and had three small boys who did the cooking and housework. His cattle were of good stuff, but very thin, and the boys thought pretty high in price, but after considerable dickering, they bought five head of the bulls for $600.00. He had wanted $150.00 apiece, but by taking as many as five, he cut a little. When they got home we were not quite ready to start, and Joe was very anxious to get back, for fear winter would set in anytime; so, as Crawford was going out with us, we told Joe to go on and we would bring the cattle, as there were only twenty-five head in all.

We got everything in shape, and about Nov. 10, we started. The weather did not look very favorable the morning we started, but we had a good tent and a cover on the wagon, plenty of bedding and buffalo robes, so we felt safe, even if it did storm. We drove the first day to a creek just north of Two-top divide and camped. Jone was not feeling well, so Crawford and I took turns on guard, and the night was pretty long. The next morning, Jone could eat no breakfast, but said he could drive the team. After a cloudy, cold morning, we got to Macy, and got a warm dinner at the house, but Jone could not eat and was no better. I told him he had better take a horse and go back, for the Cave Hills was no place for a sick man, but he said no, he would be all right in a day or two, and we started on, he in the wagon.

About two in the afternoon, it began to spit snow, and the farther we went the worse it got, but at Macy our road had turned northeast, and as the storm was from the west, it was almost to our backs, not making bad driving. It was getting colder, the snow thicker, and the wind higher, and it made me think of the time Jone and I got caught in the October storm in that same country, only a little farther on out. Late in the evening we came to Sand Creek, a little stream coming down out of the Short Pine Hills. It had considerable brush and scrub timber along its banks for shelter, and there Jone stopped to wait for us to come up. He looked about all in, and told us he had gone about as far as he could without lying down for a while. I decided we would camp there and went down the creek about a quarter of a mile where I found a fine place in a bend, well sheltered from the north and west by a high bank and brush.

We cleared the snow away, put up the tent, moved our beds in, got a nice lot of wood gathered, and prepared a warm supper, with plenty of bread to go with it mother had made for us. Jone drank a little coffee but could eat nothing.

The cattle seemed to be so well satisfied I told Crawford I would stand the first guard and if they did not try to get away we would not guard the last half of the night. It was snowing and blowing very hard, but before midnight the wind went down and I could see a few stars. The cattle had come up near the tent and lain down, so I went to bed feeling they would not leave before daylight.

The next morning it was clear but felt like it must be near zero. I got out and built a big fire right in front of the tent, and we soon had breakfast, but our bread was as hard as a bone. We had to break it in chunks and thaw it out in our coffee and the frying pan; but it was good, just the same. Jone ate a little bread and coffee but was still pretty sick. I told him if he thought he could drive, for him to go on, for the team could travel faster than the cattle, and we would get in sometime that night. We cooked more meat than we needed for breakfast and Crawford put what was left in our pockets for future use.

The snow was not drifted much and was not so very deep, so Jone pulled on ahead of us. We made good time, for the cattle did not try to stop and graze, and reached the pasture a while after dark, turned them in, and went to the ranch, which was a little more than three miles away.

Jone had gotten in about four that afternoon. He was as yellow as a duck's leg, and I did not know what to do for him, but had heard wild sage tea was good for many things, so I asked him if he would try some if I made it. He said he would try anything once, so I made him the tea, good and strong, and he drank all he could hold. He said if it didn't kill him, it surely would cure him, for it was the worst dose he had ever tasted. But he got no better, and I had to take him down in the valley where he could see a doctor.

I took him to Deadwood to Dr. Bascom Baker, a cousin of Dr. Ham Baker, and he said it was the liver causing the trouble, and he wanted to see him once a week for awhile. So we decided, as Crawford wanted to stay on the ranch, that I would go back, and Jone would stay on the river that winter.

I got enough supplies to last and went back, and when I got there, Crawford had killed a couple of black-tail deer, and he had a great time telling me just how he did it. We got up some wood, fixed up our sheds, and took about one hundred calves off the cows to wean. That was a time I always wanted to be away from home for a week, for not only did the cows and calves raise a hub-bub, but the steers would come around the corral and bawl just as loudly as the cows. We could not do much talking while around the camp, and after feeding and watering the calves, we would go and visit our neighbors.

During the summer of '91, we got a post office down the Little Missouri River below Camp Crook about eight miles, and that made it closer for our mail. It was about thirty five miles from the ranch, so by starting early, we could make the round trip in a day. The new office was called Ashcroft, after the man who kept it, and the mail came down from Camp Crook twice a week, Wednesday and

Saturday. So we arranged among ourselves to take turns going for the mail once a week and bringing it back for all the Cave Hills settlers.

My first trip came sometime in January, I do not remember the day of the month, but it was Saturday, with about two inches of snow (or frost, rather) on the ground. It was perfectly clear and very cold. I always got breakfast while Crawford fed the saddle-horses and team and milked the cows. When he came in, he said he was glad he didn't have to go for the mail, for it was the coldest morning he ever saw. I remarked there was no wind and not enough snow to make a blizzard if the wind did come up, so I was going to try it. We had no thermometer and there was no way to tell how cold it really was.

I put on yarn socks, felt boots with over-shoes, fur cap, buffalo coat, with wool-lined mittens, and started a little after sun up. I did not ride Whitie, for I could not have gotten on him with all that clothing. There was not a breath of air stirring, but I could tell it was very cold. Before I had gone five miles, there were icicles hanging from my horse's nose longer than my finger. After I got to the top of the divide, it was all level or downgrade clear to the river, and I put my horse to a 'lope nearly all the rest of the way.

I got to the post office just before noon, and one of the boys came out and put my horse in the stable for me. He was a black horse when I started that morning, but was perfectly white then.

Mr. Ashcroft said, "Man, why did you come out a day like this? If the wind had come up, you surely would have frozen. It was forty-eight below this morning."

We looked at the thermometer and it ready forty five below then, almost noon.

After we had our dinners, I told the postmaster to get all the Cave Hills mail ready, for I wanted to get home before night.

He said, "I will get the mail ready, but you are not

going back this afternoon. If the wind should come up, there is plenty of snow to make a blizzard, and if you should get lost, you would surely freeze."

It did not take much persuading to get me to stay, for the old man was an Englishman, and a very interesting man to talk to. His daughter, Alice, had taught our school one term, boarding with my parents, and I had not seen her since, until this trip. It began to cloud up in the evening and I figured I was elected to stay there through a storm. It was blowing some when we went to bed, and was a little warmer. Along towards morning I awoke and heard the wind howling, and I almost froze there under the covers thinking about my trip home; but when I came downstairs and went to feed my horse, the water was running everywhere, and the thermometer stood at 45 above, a change of 90 degrees in about eighteen hours. I know persons who have never been in the northwest would not believe such a change could come in so short a time, but I have seen it many times.

I went home that morning, and after dinner I changed horses and took the mail on over to the Dell ranch, where it was agreed the Cave Hills mail should be left. Before I got back to the ranch it was freezing, and next morning it was quite cold, but there was no snow. On this trip, I got a letter from Jone saying he thought he would go back to W. Va. on a short visit. He was not entirely well, but said Dr. Baker thought the trip would not hurt him if he behaved himself. McMaster wanted him to work for him some more, but Jone did not think it best to return to work.

All the rest of January was pretty cold, but with very little snow. Crawford had been trying for another deer, but had poor luck; so one afternoon I told him I would take that old fifty calibre rifle and try my luck. It was one of the guns Jone had brought during the Indian scare. I went up over the mountain a-foot and on the north side was plenty of deer sign, where they had been eating and lying in the buck-brush, but I saw nothing alive and started for home. When I got on top and started across the flat top of the mountain, I looked over on the edge of the cliff just above our camp and saw a yearling buck, as I thought, standing right on the edge, looking down toward the camp. I hadn't the least idea I could hit him, as he was at least 400 yards away, standing with his side to me.

I raised my sights to 400 yards, drew a bead on his shoulder, and it seemed ten seconds after the gun cracked that that deer jumped straight off the cliff. I went around to where I could get down, went to it, and instead of it being a buck, I found it to be a doe with spike horns, the only one I ever saw. I have talked to old hunters, and have never found one who ever saw a doe with spikes. The deer was not more than three hundreds yards from our dugout door. I told Crawford the deer was watching him feed the calves, and I slipped up on it.

The good people of the East used to send missionaries out to preach to us heathen, but I am afraid we did not always appreciate their kind and good intentions. Sometimes the boys would play tricks on some of them, just as though they were one of the boys. Some of those fellows were good men, and some were not so good. (Or at least the boys thought so.) I knew an old gentleman whom all the boys liked. He couldn't preach much, but he was a good man. One reason the boys all liked him was that he never beat them out of their money at poker. His name was Gardner, and he took up a homestead on Valley Creek, out near Camp Crook, about forty miles from our ranch. Another one I remember very well—he often stopped with my parents. For some cause, the boys did not like him so well, and they did play some pretty clever jokes on him. I cannot remember all of them, but I recall one.

It was before we moved our cattle north. "Brother Perry," as we all called him, had stayed all night at my father's, and about nine the next morning he started on north, going out to some of the cow-camps to beat some of the boys out of their money before they started on the roundup, I suppose. It was about the first of May and it had been raining considerably. He had to cross Owl Creek about five miles north of our place. All the streams and draws had water in them, and Owl Creek was up pretty high. He met Jone over near Owl Creek, coming south, and had asked him if he could cross the creek. Jone said, "O yes, you can cross it all right." Jone had crossed a small creek a few minutes before, and Perry could see on the horse's sides how deep it had been, so he drove on down in his two wheeled cart and went right in.

The horse started swimming, for the creek was bank full, and was one of those slow sluggish streams, ten feet deep, at least. There wasn't a good place to get out on the opposite side for at least a hundred yards below the ford. Jone told me what he had done when he got home and I said, "You should not have done that, he may get drowned."

"No," he said, "the Lord will take care of him."

A neighbor living on Indian Creek later told us Perry came to his house, and he had to give him a full change of clothes, for he had been clear under water and had lost his saddle bags and hat.

He said to the neighbor, "Why, that young Hamilton told me I could cross that creek."

"Well," Holmes said, "you did cross it, didn't you?"

I got a letter from father saying Jone had gone to W. Va., and one from my best girl telling what a good time he was having back there; but I heard nothing from him directly.

Crawford and I visited our neighbors quite often. One of Jack McKenzie's nephews came out to his ranch from Harrisburg, Pa., and he came up to see us now and then. We did not have to feed much, as there was very little snow all winter, but it kept pretty cold. Our spring up in the hills kept open, however, and we kept the ice on the creek cut in places also.

Crawford saw a porcupine in a tree one day eating bark from the limbs, and he would not go within fifty feet of it,

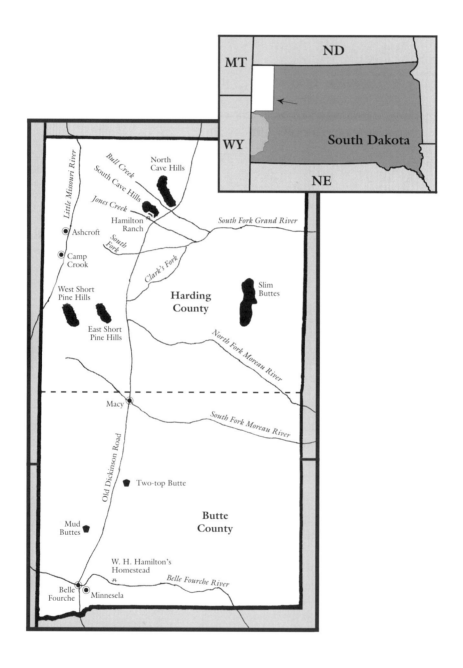

William Henry Hamilton and
Nancy Ellen Showalter
married in 1893.

Cowmen gather cattle near Belle Fourche in 1887, the summer following the
disastrous winter of 1886-1887.

Thirsty ranch hands stop for coffee at the mess camp during a cattle roundup that took place near Belle Fourche in 1887—the year W. H. Hamilton rode roundup for Minnesela rancher Asby A. Chouteau.

Branding calves required hard work and cooperation among ranch families. These cowboys are working on the plains at the edge of the Black Hills.

Hunting wolves occupied a lot of a cowman's time. Black Hills photographer John Grabill photographed these cowboys and their captive gray wolf on a roundup in eastern Wyoming.

The scenic beauty of the Cave Hills formed the backdrop of cowman W. H. Hamilton's life.

The town of Minnesela, photographed in about 1890, was the home community of the homesteading Hamiltons, but Minnesela faded with the rise of its neighbor and rival, Belle Fourche.

By 1901, Hamilton's growing family led him to move to a more settled area. Pictured left to right are W. H., Sarah Lucretia (Walthall), William Jackson, Nancy Ellen, and Ray Showalter Hamilton.

"For," he said, "they can throw their quills fifty feet or more." I told him they could throw their quills just as far as they could reach with their tail.

In March we had a wet snow that drifted our cattle to the south side of our pasture and after we got them back, we fed them a couple of loads of hay per day until the ground was bare again. We kept bringing cows with young calves into the shed, where we could feed them hay, for some of them were pretty thin after rustling all winter.

The weather got nice in April and we did not have to feed any. We turned the calves out, so we had nothing much to do, and one nice day we decided to go down to the E6 ranch and see the boys.

The cowboys were hunting jobs for the summer, so we had plenty of company. It was about fifteen miles down Jones Creek to the E6. When we got there, we found the boys getting their saddles and bridles, ropes and spurs, in shape for work.

They had one old red horse that had the habit of lying down when they first saddled him. He would lie flat on the ground sometimes for a half hour before he would get up, and it was no use trying to get him up until he got his nap out.

Someone said, "Let's saddle Red and see if he has forgotten his trick."

One of the boys threw his rope on him, and down he went, flat on his side. There was a boy among the bunch, about sixteen I guess. His name was Robinson—Buster, they called him. He was standing around not saying much. He was wanting a job, but Joe had been putting him off.

After a while he said, "Why don't you make that old horse get up?"

"I would like to see you make him get up," he was told.

He said, "I can." And then the boys all began to "guy" him and wanted to bet him money.

"You know I have no money, but I can make him get up," he said.

Tom Williams had ridden the horse the summer before and knew him well. He spoke up and said, "Buster, if you make Red get up, I will give you a five-dollar William."

The boy said nothing but started off toward the ranch-house, and after a bit he came down to the corral carrying a great big old tom-cat in his arms. No one said anything, but just watched Buster. He walked around to old Red's back, took the cat by the tail, dropped him right over under Red's flank, and gave a pull, you out to have seen that horse—I don't think I ever saw a horse 'light on all four feet as quickly. Tom went over to Buster, handed him over the fiver and said, "I have paid five dollars many times to learn a trick that was not half as good as that."

And at dinner, when the boys told Joe, the foreman, he said, "Buster, you are hired and you shall have Red in your string."

Buster asked, "Shall we take the cat on the roundup?"

The boys wanted us to stay all night, but we went on home that afternoon. In a few days Jone went on out to the ranch, and we broke a few horses. Crawford was a big strong fellow, and a mighty good fellow to have around. He rode pretty well for the practice he had, but would not get on a horse he thought would buck. But a fellow can help in breaking horses in more ways than in riding them.

The last half of April was pretty wet, and a good time to break horses, as the ground was soft and they would tire quickly. We got about seven or eight so one man could saddle them, and that is called "broke."

Jone had lots to tell me about the folks back East, and the changes that the people had made. He had not been back there since he left there in the summer of '84. He insisted that the people had changed very much, but I found later when I was back that we were the ones who had done the changing. We had fallen into the ways and habits of the West, while they were going on in their same old way back in the Blue Ridges.

Crawford and I went down to the settlement and he went on to Lead City, where he got work in the mines. J. C. Dennison's school was out and he had decided he was not cut out for a stockman. So he went to Quincy, Ill., to a business college. He took a two year course, and Mr. Musselman, the president, got him a job in Kansas City, where he still lives. He sold his cattle to Will Shaw, McKenzie's nephew.

While hunting up on the mountain at different times, I saw where holes had been dug in the ground. They were all about four feet square and three feet deep, with sticks laid across the top, covered with dry grass. They were always out on a point, next to the rim-rock. I asked McKenzie what it meant. He said the Indians made them to catch eagles, so they could get the feathers. They would get down in the hole, with a jackrabbit on top for bait, and when the eagle would swoop down on the rabbit, they would reach up and catch him and jerk the tail and wing feathers all out. They are superstitious, and will not kill an eagle, but will take his feathers and turn him loose to starve.

But the Indian was not alone in doing things which seemed to bear a touch of cruelty. The stockman was sometimes placed in hard and difficult positions, and sometimes had to do things that looked cruel. To illustrate, I will relate the experience of one of my neighbors and I. Charlie Schlosser and I had adjoining homesteads on the river, and he and his partner also had a horseranch on Owl Creek. He lived on his homestead during the winter, and was on the horse ranch most of the summer. Charlie came to me one day in the summer of '89 and said, "How busy are you, Bill?"

I said, "Not so busy but that I can help a friend. What is it?"

He said he had three or four fillies which had left the bunch the winter before and that Billy Moses said he thought he saw them in a renegade bunch on the Owl Creek and Little Missouri River divide. He could not get close enough to see the brand, but the way he described them, Charlie thought they might be his. He said he knew one man could do nothing with them.

For the benefit of those who are not used to the western range, I will say that renegade horses are headed by a young stallion which has been run out of his own bunch by the older stallion. He picks up any mares or fillies that will follow him, and they soon become very wild and hard to handle.

Charley said it might require three or four days to do the job. He asked me if I had a very fast horse. I said no, but that I had one that could go as long as the next one. He said that that was what it would take.

So the next morning we pulled out and went to a line camp on the head of Owl Creek, and stayed with the line rider, E. A. Stambaugh, a neighbor boy. The next day we took until noon before we sighted them.

Charlie said, "That is the bunch. Now we will go on down the river and find a place to corral them. I know where there is a round-up corral right on the bank of the river, and if it is in good repair, there is where we will take them."

This corral was in a nice smooth flat and for about a half mile up the river, the bank was very high so nothing could cross the river. That gave us the advantage, if we ever got them headed that way. A wing had been built from the corral out across the bottom some distance from the river.

So we went back and soon found the horses, not far from where we first saw them, twelve in all, and they were young, fast, and wild. When they first started, I didn't think we could ever do a thing with them, but Charlie was a real horseman and I took orders from him. We circled, and one would turn them on divide, and the other head them on another, and always kept them headed toward the river.

Finally we got them down on the river bottom. Our horses were hot, but they had gotten their second wind, were on their mettle, and we were closing in on them.

At last they made a break for the river bank, I on the up-river side, and Charlie cutting in on the wing when they struck the river. I had them pointed down stream and that led them right in behind the wing. It was short work to then force them on into the corral, put up the bars, and begin to take note of what we had.

The stallion was as pretty a little horse as I ever saw —a bright bay with black mane and tail. Charlie had three fillies in the bunch, and the stallion was one which had gotten away from T. P. Harrison on the Bullock ranch near Minnesela. He was a Kentucky Thoroughbred, so no wonder he could run!

Charlie said, "We are in luck if we can ever get that horse home, for Harrison has been looking for him for two years. He is now four years old."

I said, "If we turn that horse and your fillies out of here, we cannot keep in sight of them, and they will all get away."

"Well," he said, "those fillies will follow that stallion through a fire, but what can we do to keep him from running off?"

When we got them all looked over, there was a fillie in the bunch with Harrison's brand also. That made five we wanted. Well, it was almost sundown, so we decided to leave them until morning. Charlie said he knew of a cow camp not more than five or six miles up the river, so we tied the bars with one of our ropes to be sure of them, and galloped up the river to get some grub, for we were both very hungry. We found the place, and all the boys were gone on the roundup, but there was plenty of food. We got supper and it took considerable to fill us.

After supper I said, "I believe I have a plan that will hold that horse so we can drive him, and he will not get away."

"What will we do, hobble him?" Charlie asked.

I said, "No. We can't drive him that way. You are the boss, and if you think my plan is not practical, we won't do it. I think the only way is to tie one of those fillies to his tail."

He said, "That will be pretty rough on the filly, but I think like you, that it is the only way we will ever get that horse to Harrison."

Next morning, after we got breakfast, we went down and they were still there. Charlie was a good roper, so he lassoed the horse, we pulled his feet from under him, and tied him down. I said as it was Harrison's horse, I supposed we could use his filly as a rudder. So we caught her and tied her down, but she fell about a rod from the horse.

Charlie said, "Well, we have them down and tied, but we must tie her up close to him so she can't get over the rope."

I said, "Make a hackamore out of that rope we stole at the ranch and I will bring Old Fox in here and we will have her in position shortly."

I brought my horse in, took the hackamore rope, wrapped it around the saddle horn, and pulled the filly up astern the stallion, tying her head close up. Then we cut out the bunch we did not want, put the bars up, took the rope off the filly's feet, and I held her down until Charlie loosed the rope on the horse. They both came to their feet at once, and that horse swung her around pretty lively for awhile. After they got a little used to it we opened the bars, got on our horses, and out we went, the filly hitting only the high places for about a mile. Then they quieted down and drove fine. We corraled them at an old corral on Owl Creek that night and got them home next day; and that filly was well-broke to lead, and the horse was pretty tame also.

We had the horses all out at the ranch now, and father said he would like to stay at the cow-ranch part of the summer. He had proved up on his homestead the fall before.

Our neighbor, Alex Connell, had brought in a small bunch of Percheron mares about three years before, but had had bad luck with them.

There was some loco-weed on Bull Creek, and some of them got some of it. When a horse gets loco, he hunts for more of it and will do no good from then on. Connell wanted us to take the mares on shares, as we had a good Percheron horse—we to keep the mares in our pasture where there was no loco, and get half shares.

So father took a team, led the Percheron, and went out to the ranch, taking enough supplies to last until time to put up hay. Uncle Will and Alden, his son, moved their cattle to the Cave Hills that spring and located on the northeast side side near the cave, about fifteen miles from us. J. B. McVey and his two boys settled on the north side of the Hills the same summer, so the hill country was getting pretty well settled up.

I put out a small crop of corn on the homestead, but no small grain. It had been so dry for the last three seasons small grain was almost a failure. In the summer of '92 a good many of our neighbors got discouraged, mortgaged their claims for all they could, and left them; and many of them never came back. Consequently, our school began to run down.

I sent a man out in July with a load of shingles, lumber, and supplies, to help put up hay. Isaac Arpan had been looking after the cattle while father and Jone had been working on our log house, and they had it all ready for the roof when the shingles and lumber came. Father was a good hand at hewing and raising a log house, as he had been reared in the mountains of Virginia where most of the houses were made of logs.

About the first of September, my sister and cousin Orpha Hamilton, wanted to go out to the ranch and get plums, and to visit the two Hamilton ranches. I rigged up an old buckboard we had and gave them two old plug cowhorses that we had worked some, and they pulled out, making the trip out in two days without mishap. They visited at both places, gathered plums, and had a good time in general, especially Orpha, as she had never been out there before.

Just after the girls got out to the ranch, the boys having finished the hay and the two hands wanting to come home, Jone sent them down with a team so I could come out with some more lumber and be at the ranch while Jone was gone with the shipment of beef.

But things do not always go the way we plan them. The girls started one morning to come home, but just as they were starting down the hill from the ranch house, one tug came unhooked on the old buckskin horse, the end of the single-tree flew back in the spokes of the wheel and scared him, he made a jump forward, letting the tongue come down, and away they went, throwing the girls out, turning the buckboard over. They pulled out across the pasture, and when the run was over, they could not get enough pieced together to make another buckboard.

Well, it was decided father would hitch the old ponies to a wagon and bring Orpha home, as her school was to start soon, and sister was to stay at the ranch with Jone until I came out. I was supposed to be there before Jone started with the beef.

I was not quite ready when father and Orpha got home but got ready in a day or so and started out.

After father started home, the Bull Creek fellows decided to start a day or two sooner than had at first been planned, so some of the boys helped Jone round up and cut out our beef, and they left two days before I got there, sister holding down the ranch alone in the meantime. I got to the ranch near midnight the second day and found sister sleeping in the hay-corral. She said she did not want to be cornered in a dugout, but was not afraid out in the open as long as she had a good six-shooter to defend her.

In a day or two sister started home. I gave her a good

horse, although he was a little hard to get on. I went with her to the south gate of the pasture, let her out, and told her to go straight south to the west side of a butte I pointed out to her, so she would come into the road at South Grand River and save about three miles. But she kept too far west and crossed the river above the ford, getting into the badlands where she could not make time and did not get into the road until she got on top of the divide between Clark's Fork and Moreau River, not getting to Macy until about ten that night. She visited with the Oliver girls the next day and went on home the day after.

I was busy putting the roof on the house and looking after the cattle until Jone got back. The boys elected Jone foreman on the drive that fall, as we had more cattle in the herd than anyone else. He said the grass was good most of the way and the weather was fine until the night before they got to Dickinson.

There was a black cloud in the northwest that evening, and they could see a little flash of lightning occasionally when they went to bed. Curliss went with the herd that fall instead of his son. He was the oldest man in the bunch, so Jone said he most always put him on the last guard, as it was usually easiest. He said he was on guard himself just before Mr. Curliss, and the cloud had gotten up closer, but it was not thundering any, and was not very dark when he came in and wakened the old man. The cattle had been so quiet they had been using only one man at guard at a time. He said he had not been asleep but a short time until he awoke and heard the old man squalling like a Sioux Indian. He called the boys and they all got their horses and broke for the herd. When they got there, the old fellow was going around the herd at break-neck speed and the electricity was running off those steers horns in streaks, and they were milling round and round. He said the sparks would even fly off the horse's ears, and once, when the old man passed him, he was grabbing at the sparks that were running off his long mustache. He said that for about thirty minutes, it was about the most exciting time he ever saw, and the strange thing about it was, there was no thunder at all with the electricity.

Jone went on to Chicago with the cattle. Our herd weighed well, but the price was not so good as the fall before. The best was $4.00, the others about $3.75 and cows $2.40, but we had no reason to complain, as they sold in the same class as the cornfed cattle from the corn belt, and had not cost us anything near what those had.

When Jone got back, I had the roof on the house. We then put down the floor, made the partition, and chinked in and daubed it with good old gumbo, and it was ready to move into. We hauled up a nice lot of ash and pine wood, for we knew we would have to use a lot more fuel than we did in the dugout.

We had a lot of young chickens which had hatched out in the weeds and had almost raised themselves, and as we did not want to haul grain all the way from the river to feed more than we needed, and they were hardly worth hauling all the way down to Belle Fourche as they sold at that time for about $2.25 per dozen, we decided to eat them. As we were busy, we would kill and cook two of them a night at first, and eat them next day. At the beginning, we could clean up two each day, as we both were very fond of chicken. But it was not long until one did us for two days and it grew worse all the time. Finally it got so it made cold chills run over me to get one ready to cook, to say nothing about staying in the house while it was cooking. I do not know how brother Jone is, but I got enough chicken to do me the rest of my life.

We never lost any chickens by coyotes catching them, as they would not come up in the canyon where our buildings were. A coyote is a very sly and cunning animal, almost always travelling with a mate, and when they go to cross a hollow or gulch, one will always stop back on high ground so it can see around the country until the other crosses, then they will go on their way. They will never go inside of a building.

Well, we got our cattle all inside, our work all up, sheds fixed, and everything ready for winter. We now had as good a house as any in the Hills and were ready to live like white folks. I was out of debt and owned a third interest in a good bunch of cattle and horses, and I was wanting to see the girl I had left in the mountains of Virginia, to find out for sure whether she was ready to give up a good job teaching school in a civilized community for an ordinary cow-puncher on the frontier of South Dakota. Of course, we had been exchanging letters, and I had told her as nearly as I could just how things were out there but I was afraid she did not quite understand the situation and it would be terrible to take her out there and she not having realized the kind of place it was until she got there. So I asked Jone if I sent a man out in my place, did he think he could get along.

He said, "Sure, go ahead. If you stayed here you would be gone to the post office most of the time anyway."

He went out and killed four or five deer a day or so before I started, and I took two them them and a half of a beef we had killed, and a lot of those left-over chickens, and pulled for the river. I hunted up Jack Billue, the boy who had worked for us that summer, got the supplies for the winter, and Jack took the team I had driven in and went back to the ranch to stay for the winter.

I helped father get up enough wood to last all winter, and about the middle of December, I bought a ticket for Grafton, W. Va. We had had some pretty cold weather before I started East but with very little snow. When I got to W. Va., it was nice and warm, but it rained almost every day, which made it very muddy and disagreeable. I would much rather had had zero weather.

I found everybody well, and they all appeared to be glad to see me. I went to Uncle Jim Hamilton's for it always seemed more like home than anywhere else. Oran was at home for the winter and knew where to go to have a good time, as the young folks always let him know about all that was going on.   My best girl only lived one mile from my uncle's place.

Oran and I took in all the protracted meetings up in the mountain section and there was always one going on somewhere in reach, for they never thought of one lasting less than a month, and if they got one going just right and the excitement running pretty high, they usually lasted six weeks.

Some of my old mountain friends were much surprised to see me, for they had gotten the news that we had been all killed by the Indians; not only killed, but also scalped. To be sure, Jone had been back there the winter before, but news does not travel very fast back in the mountains, and when they once hear a thing, it lasts a long time.

As our relatives were spread over a considerable portion of two or three counties, it took some time to get around, and the first thing I knew, the winter was about gone.

I spent considerable time at one Miss Showalter's home, and at her boarding place, for she was teaching near Philippi, and when the word got out that I was trying to take her back to Dakota with me, I was always careful to have some of my friends with me when at any parties, for some of her friends talked like they might mob a fellow who would take a girl to such a place as they had heard Dakota was. And when she gave up her school and came they were sure that it was so, that she was going with that cowboy!

So, on Feb. 5th, '93, Miss Nancy Ellen Showalter and "that cowboy" were married and began to make plans for the future.

I had not been over in Tucker Co. yet to see my uncle, Smith Dennison, and his family. I knew they would want to hear about their boys, John and J. C. John was still in Dakota, while J. C. had gone to Quincy. Crawford also wanted me to go see his people. They lived about seven miles up the river from Beverly, W. Va. So we went to see the Denisons, and after we got back we went to Philippi to visit my wife's sister and family. I then went on to see the Crawfords, hiring a horse at a livery stable in Beverly. I spent Sunday with them and told them all about their son and I, staying together the winter before on the cow ranch. I talked with them all day and told them everything I knew about the country, its climate, products, and its people, both white and red; and when I started back to Beverly, the old gentleman was still asking for more, and said he was certainly glad I came to see them.

When I got back to Beverly, I found that I had hired my horse from a man who had married a second cousin of mine, and we had not seen each other since we were about eight years old. So there was no getting away from there until the next day. When I got back to Philippi, I found the wife very uneasy, thinking something had happened to me because I had stayed overtime, but it was not long until she got used to that and never looked for me until she saw me.

We started for Dakota about March 10, and were met by my father in Belle Fourche, who took us down to the ranch in a road-wagon. My wife wanted to bring her organ, so we had boxed and shipped it before we started, but it had not gotten to Belle Fourche yet. So we loaded ourselves and trunks into the wagon and went down to my parents for a while. It was not yet safe to start for the ranch, and we decided to stay until spring opened up.

I did not think much about what my wife was undertaking at the time, but I have many times since. She must have had lots of faith in me to do what she did; and she had not only faith, but lots of courage. I know there are but few women who would or could have done a similar thing.

We did not start out to the ranch until about the middle of April. The weather stayed rough, and the ground soft, and I knew that if we got caught on the gumbo and it began to roll, there was but one thing to do—stop and camp. That gumbo is queer stuff. I have seen men who were not accustomed to it drive out of the road when it began to roll up on the wheel. That is the worst thing to do, as it will pick up the grass, which acts like hair in old-style plaster—makes it roll faster—and it can hardly be gotten off. When I was alone, I did not mind, but I did not want my wife caught in any such scrape so early in her new undertaking.

There was a country store and post office just across the river from my father's and it was customary about forty years ago for young couples to have some photos taken with their uniforms on. Well, we had followed the old custom, and the photos were not finished when we started home. So I had them sent to us by mail. I was over to the office one day, and the postmistress handed me a package and said "I bet that is the pack of pictures of you and your wife."

I said, "I think so."

She said, "Open them up. I want to see what kind of a looking wife you've got."

She looked at them awhile, and then at me.

"Why," she said, "You look alike!"

"Well," I said, "I am not surprised, for my aunt was her grandmother!"

I did not take the trouble to tell her that my aunt was her step-grandmother.

Well, it soon got started that Virginia Bill had married a near relation and I never denied it.

The weather got settled somewhat, and about April 15, we loaded the organ and what few other housekeeping articles we had, with plenty of grub, into the wagon. I always thought more about having plenty to eat than having furniture. If I had enough to eat, I could sit down on the ground Indian fashion and eat it, rather than have a mahogany table and an overstuffed chair and nothing to chew on.

We went to Fasberrys' on Indian Creek the first evening,

so we could make it to Macy the next day. Next morning it was cloudy, but I knew it was too cold to rain, and I was glad of it, for it was my worst gumbo country from Indian Creek to Macy. We got along fine that day, and stopped on Dry Creek just north of Two-top divide to feed our team and eat dinner. I gathered buffalo-chips and made a good fire to boil our coffee and warm ourselves, for it was pretty cold. My wife said that was the first time she had ever seen coffee made over that kind of stuff and she did not know whether it was fit to drink or not, but admitted that it tasted rather good anyway. I told her that was one good thing about driving over the prairie, one was always hungry enough to eat anything he could get.

We got to Macy about dark and had a good warm supper and after supper there were several young fellows who had come in for the mail, and the two Oliver girls, so with my wife and I, we had a pretty good crowd. As the girls had an organ and we were all fairly good singers, and some of us could play the mouth harp, we all had a real good time. The "missus" was getting acquainted with the young folks of the West.

Next morning it was somewhat colder and looked like snow, but as we had a good cover on the wagon and as the wind was rather to our backs, we started. We had not gone more than three miles until it began to snow and kept getting worse, and by the time we had gone eight miles, we couldn't see a hundred yards. I knew where the Zoelker Bros. cow-ranch was—only about three miles off the road. When we came to the place to turn off I said we had better go down to the ranch and stay until the storm was over. My wife did not like the idea of going to a bachelor ranch, but said to do what I thought best; and I knew it would be best for us to turn in and put up with the boys. By the time we got to the ranch, it was terrible.

There were three boys at the ranch. One of them, Elmer Stambaugh, was a near neighbor on the river. The boys came out and helped get the team in out of the storm, we got in by a good fire, and were glad we were so lucky.

After dinner, one of the boys saw the organ in the wagon and nothing would do but that we must bring it into the house. Stambaugh was a pretty good fiddler, and the Missus could second very well, so we had plenty of music that afternoon. The boys were very nice, and it was but a little while until my wife felt as much at home as if she had been among her own kind of people.

She was amused at the way the boys cooked. She asked to help get supper, and they did let her make the biscuits. She often laughs yet at the way the boys set the table. One stood at the cupboard and tossed the plates to their places on the table. They bounced around considerably, but always settled down in the right places. I do not know how long he had practiced that stunt to become so efficient. Of course they were tin plates.

The storm kept raging all day and on into the night, but it was not very cold. The boys made us a bedroom by hanging a tarpaulin across an end of the one room of the house .

Next morning it was clear and bright, with no ground in sight. Although the thermometer was not very low, I was afraid to start because of the danger of snowblindness. March and April are the worst months for this trouble, and I am more afraid of snow-blindness than of a blizzard. So we stayed over until the next morning, when the snow had settled and melted so we could see the ground in a few places. It would be a full day's drive, so we loaded the organ back into the wagon and started a little after sunup.

When we got on top of the divide between North Moreau and Clark's Fork, I stopped the team to show my wife where our future home was to be, for a time at least, and to let her see the wonderful mud buttes that were scattered over a scope of country of about five by eight miles. The Cave Hills show like a mountain range from this divide, and only seem to be about five miles away, but are a good twenty-five.

Those mud buttes are about the strangest earth formation I have ever seen. From this divide, the area looks like a large meadow covered with hay ricks of all shapes and sizes. Some are round, some are long, like a very long haystack, and some are shaped like a house; but all are somewhere near the same height. The country they are in is a prairie, almost entirely level, and the soil is a mixed sand and gumbo. There is not one bit of vegetation growing within fifty feet of the base of any of them. The buttes are mostly of a yellow clay formation, and in lots of them, one can find petrified wood from a few inches in length to more than twenty feet. One butte in particular, about one fourth mile east of the old road is rather a double one, about one hundred and fifty feet and one hundred feet through at the base. Time and weather have worn a notch in the middle of it down some twenty-five or thirty feet, and it shows a petrified tree about 25 feet long, the ends running back into the butte no telling how far. The tree is more than a foot in diameter, and it shows plainly where limbs have been. It would pay anyone to go a long way to see this place.

After we rested our team and looked at the buttes for some time, we went on and got to the ranch about dark. We found the boys getting along fine, and glad to see us. The next day we got everything placed around, and started house keeping.

The cattle had come through the winter in good condition. The bachelors all came to see us, as they wanted to see what kind of a looking lady Bill had tricked into marrying him. And she was the only woman in the Hills at that time, as Mrs. Dell had gone to her parents in Iowa the fall before and would not be back until late summer.

We had some saddle horses to break, so we got at that as soon as we could. They were all big and wild. I had a good gentle horse for the missus, and she was out with us most of the time. It was not long until she could haze a horse as well as either of us, and she seemed to fall right in with the ways of the range.

We had a fine garden spot not more than fifty yards from the house. We put out a lot of seeds, and my wife set some eggs, so we would have chicken to eat. I told her to raise what she thought she and the hired man could handle, as Jone and I had had enough the fall before to do us for all time. It was not long then until the antelope were fat, and from then on we had plenty of fresh meat. There were some mountain sheep in the Hills, but we had never been able to get one. I had a fair shot at one that spring, but was too anxious and missed him.

Cousin Will Hamilton was working for Dell for the summer. We had gotten five horses broken so one man could saddle them, but they were green and wild yet. Jone wanted to go down and see his girl and Jack planned to go home for a while, so they each took a young horse and that left me three of the green ones to finish breaking. I had plenty of work for them, for it was in the spring that the cattle were hardest to hold. It meant about a twenty-five mile ride every day, besides the range cattle to throw back off our range. So of mornings I would saddle a horse and the wife would haze us out on the open range and we were gone until afternoon. We kept some excitement going all the time, and my wife got to see new country and had new experiences every day. One Sunday we decided not to ride after cattle, but to go over and see Will and Mr. Dell, and find out when Mrs. Dell would be home. I caught a horse I had not ridden for a few days, but I was not able to get the saddle on him until my wife came to my assistance. I finally got him snubbed up, and by her help, got him blind-folded. Then it was easy to saddle him. I told her to get on her horse, and keep mine out of the wire fence until we got to the open. I left the blind on until I was in the saddle, then she rode by and pulled it off, and then the fun began. He went high in the air, in circles, and all kinds of ways, until finally we got started for the open range, and after about a two mile run, he settled down and all was smooth going. We got to the Dell ranch and found no one at home. I knew they were out after cattle and would be home by noon, so we put our horses in the corral and before long,

Will came in. He and my wife then started getting dinner. After a while Dell came and we had a nice visit. Dell said he was looking for his wife and little boy home in July.

It was about ten miles the way we had come, round the mountain, but going back, we cut off about four miles by going up through the rim-rock and over. The June berry and plum bushes were all in full bloom in the canyons, making a very beautiful sight.

One day along in June I asked the missus if she would like to see some of the fine springs around the mountain inside the pasture. She said she would, so I took the Winchester and we walked, it being about a mile up to the spring. I wanted her to see the water where it came off the top of about a two-foot vein of coal. Here it would not freeze in the coldest weather until it had run a rod or more from where it came out of the ground. She had not seen any deer yet, but while we were looking at the spring and tasting the water, I looked along the mountain side and saw six deer watching us, but they were a little too far away to give me a good shot. We started to sneak up a little closer, but they took flight and ran. I said if we climbed up the cliff and ran across the point I might get a shot yet. We did so, and just as we came out on the rimrock, they came by about one hundred and fifty yards away, but almost straight under us, and I suppose I over shot them. At least, I did not get one, but she got to see a nice bunch of black-tail, or mule deer. She had already seen plenty of antelope, coyotes, rattlesnakes and jackrabbits.

I have said very little about rattlesnakes, I suppose because they are so plentiful. While riding after cattle during the summer, I scarcely ever missed killing from one to four or five a day. I always carried a quirt on the saddle horn and used it to clip off their heads. I never got in such a hurry that I would not stop and kill one when I heard it rattle. I had read about how far they would jump to strike, but that is all hog-wash. They cannot even strike their length. They are not a very long snake, very seldom reaching three feet, and they have a button for the first year and a rattle for each year thereafter. They always give a rattle warning before striking. They were very thick along the edge of the hills in the spring, but got out on the prairie during the summer. We did not have much stock bitten by them. I remember that one of our work horses got bitten on the nose once and when I found him, his head was terribly swollen. He could not shut his mouth and both eyes were entirely closed. I got cacti and split them, binding the raw side to the bite, and changed them every half hour, and in twelve hours the swelling was reduced so he could see and drink. We lost one cow by snake bite, as we did not find her in time.

There was going to be a big celebration and dance at Minnesela, and my wife had not seen a woman since we got to the ranch, so we thought we would take that in. I wanted to take two wagons down to bring out lumber, so she drove one and I drove the other, and we made the trip down in two days, were there for the big event, and stayed for the dance that night.

I had to go up in the Black Hills for the lumber. Father and I went. It was raspberry time and they were plentiful. We loaded our loads and spent the rest of our time picking berries, staying at the mill overnight.

Mother said she would like to go out and visit with us for a while. I got Jack Billue to help us thru the haying. He drove one wagon and I the other, and having tent and camping outfit, we pulled out the tenth of July. The first night out, we camped on Two-top divide, and the wind blew some all night so the mosquitoes did not bother badly. But the next night we were on Duck Creek, about ten miles northeast of Macy, and about the time we were eating supper, the wind went down. Before long it was hard work to keep the mosquitoes out of our mouths. We staked the tent tightly to the ground and put the women folks in, shut the tent up tight and Jack and I slept on top of the lumber, or rather stayed on top of the lumber. Our horses rolled and fought mosquitoes all night, and we did the same. In the morning we started early to make the ranch that day.

The wind came up about eight o'clock, giving us a little rest from our aggressors. We got in by sundown, and were glad to get up in the hills, where the mosquitoes were never nearly so bad as on the prairie.

We got home just in time for the June berry harvest, and we spent a good part of our time among the bushes, serving berries in all styles. Jone had killed a nice fat antelope the day before we got home, and the young sage hens were ripe, so we had plenty to eat. Young potatoes were large enough to use, and peas were ready in the garden.

We got our haywagons rigged up and began making hay about July 20. Jone went with the E6 on the round-up for awhile.

Jack and I were making hay up toward the top of the divide, and one day I saw the smoke from a fire over toward the little Missouri. It was near noon. I told Jack to take the two teams on one load of hay and I would go to the fire. I always kept a saddle horse with me.

It was a very hot day, but the wind was not blowing when I got to the fire, over the divide about three miles. There was a bunch of cowboys already there, but they were not making much headway. One of the boys said he saw a crippled steer down below a short distance.

I asked, "Where is your cook wagon?"

They told me about two miles on down the river.

I said, "Send one of your boys down to get an ax, and while he is gone we will kill the steer, and we will soon put this fire out if the wind does not come up."

When the boy got back, one of the boys had killed the animal. We split it in two pieces lengthwise and I put a saddle rope on one front leg, while another boy put his rope on the hind leg of the same half; then two other lads got the other half rigged up the same way, and we went to the fire. When we got there, one pair went one way, and one the other, on the line of fire with the raw side down. When

the wind is not blowing, a prairie fire can be put out in that
way as fast as a horse can walk. We had that fire all out
within two hours after I got there.

Jone got home from the roundup and we went at the hay
with a rush. We had a pretty good crop that year. Father
came down and got mother sometime in August. Mrs. Dell
came home about the first of September, and Charley Vansickle, who lived at Table Mountain, got married and brought
his wife home. So you see the country was filling up with
women.

The wife and I went up to see the Vansickles one Sunday,
and just after we crossed Bull Creek, we saw a big bunch
of antelope, twenty-five or thirty in number. It was the
largest bunch my wife had ever seen. She got to see some
new country, also, and we both enjoyed our visit.

The next day my right hand began to pain me, and I
could not sleep that night. It kept getting worse and finally
developed into a felon on the second finger. It swelled as
large as two fingers should be, and I could neither eat nor
sleep. After I had suffered for more than a week, I told my
wife I could stand it no longer, and would have to go to
Belle Fourche to have the thing lanced. The boys had gone
to the hayfield, and as it was my right hand affected, I did
not know if I could put the saddle on a horse, for my saddle
weighed fifty pounds; but my wife said she could saddle him,
so I drove the horses in the corral, and by her help, caught
and saddled a good gentle horse. About ten in the morning
I started out, and she went to the south gate to let me out.
My hand hurt so much I could not let it down, or even carry
it by my side in a sling, so I carried it above my head most
all the way to Macy. I got there about sundown and thought
I would stay there that night, for the horse needed the rest.
Macy said he had some pills which would ease the pain,
that his wife took them. He kept giving them to me until
he said I did not dare take any more, but they did not ease
the pain, and about nine that night, Macy saddled my horse
and the next morning at daylight, I was in Belle Fourche,
routing the doctor out of bed. He took me down to his

office and split that finger plenty, and in ten minutes after-wards I believe I felt better than I ever did in my life. I went to the restaurant and got my breakfast, the first meal I had eaten with any satisfaction for more than a week. I then went down the river eight miles to my father's and told mother I wanted to lie down for a nap, but not to waken me until I had my nap out. I knew nothing more until after midnight.

Next day I went back to the doctor to have the finger dressed, and mailed a letter that sister had written to my wife, so she would know I was getting along all right. The doctor said he wanted to see the finger the next day. I went back then, and he said it was doing all right, but not to go back to the ranch for two or three days yet, for it might close up and give me trouble. But I knew my wife would be very uneasy about me, for it was not certain she would get the letter and the boys would be away from the ranch all day, leaving her alone most of the time. So the next day I started home, putting up at Macy that night, where I got the letter sister had written, and went on to the ranch the next day.

My wife said she had been looking for me for the last two days. Each evening she watched the gap in the mountain to the south with the field glasses until it got too dark to see.

The boys had gotten along well with the hay and it was drawing near shipping time. I could do nothing but ride after the cattle, and either my wife or one of the boys went on circle with me, taking until nearly noon.

My hand closed up and began to pain again in a few days after I got home. I had to carry it in a sling all the time, and there was a red streak running from my finger to my shoulder. It hurt me very badly all the time, and the doctor told me afterwards that he was surprised I didn't get blood poisoning. I could not use my hand to do any good until almost winter.

While I was still carrying my hand in a sling, brother

Jone and I were gathering cattle and turning them into the pasture. It was a raw, windy day, and we were in south of the mountain. We had gathered quite a bunch, and while coming up the slope toward the west end of the mountain, Jone said, "If you will head this bunch around to the west side, I will go down through the rough ground and see if any are in there, and meet you over at the west gate."

He had not been gone but a few minutes until I saw a big mountain sheep come up out of the rough ground and come straight toward the cattle, then right on through the herd toward me. I could not resist the temptation to take after him. I was riding Fox, my old standby, and I knew we could run circles around the sheep. How I did wish Jone was there! I ran right up on him and could have caught him with a ten-foot rope. I circled him around on the flat until I had all that kind of fun I wanted, and then let him go and started on after the cattle. I had not got back to the herd until I saw Jone come out of the badlands throwing his overcoat as he came, but the sheep was then out of sight.

We rounded up the beef and the boys started south with them about the 20th of September, as we were shipping from Belle Fourche that fall. Jack stayed with me to help look after the cattle, for on some days, I was unable to ride. While Jone was gone with the cattle my wife fell sick and I did not know what to do. Mrs. Dell had come back to the ranch late that summer, so I went for her, and she came and stayed a week, doing everything she could for her, but she got no better. Jone got home about Oct. 10 and brought our mother with him. Father went to Chicago with the cattle, as he wanted to go to the Exposition.

After mother came, my wife still did not improve, and finally I started Jack to Belle Fourche for a doctor. He took a good horse and made the trip down in twenty-four hours, but could get no doctor there, so he went on to Spearfish, where he got a doctor and a fellow to bring him with a livery team. He stayed down a few days to rest his horse.

The doctor drove day and night to get to the ranch.

When he got there he said she was a pretty sick woman, but not dangerously so and would be better soon. He stayed the rest of that day and night and started back the next morning. I do not remember his name, but I do remember that I paid him $150.00 and felt it was worth it to know she was not seriously ill. She got somewhat better, and after a few days we thought it best for her to go down to the settlement before winter set in, so we fixed a bed in the covered wagon, as she could not sit up, and I took her and mother down home. Jack was to stay on the ranch with Jone.

After we got home, my wife got better, but I knew she had gone through a trying summer, and we both thought it would be best for her if she went back to W. Va. and spent the winter. I went with her to Whitewood, where she had to change trains.

Father had gotten home, having sold the steers for $4.00 and the cows at $2.25 per hundred, and they weighed well. Father had had a good trip, spending a few days at the fair. I took the winter supplies and went back to the ranch. Jack came home, and by this time, winter had set in. We had the cattle all in, the boys had the calves weaned, and I was glad of it. The boys had killed some venison, and with a fresh beef, we were well supplied with meat.

Alden Hamilton had married that summer, but had not brought his wife out to the ranch. Jone and I kept pretty busy looking after the cattle and horses. The wolves had killed a few colts and a couple of yearlings during the summer. There was a den over on the head of Grand River, about six or seven miles southwest. We had tried to poison them, but with no success, getting coyotes, but no wolves. Wolves are very hard to trap or poison. In fact it takes an expert to catch them with anything except with good dogs.

Bill Shaw's brother John had come out from Pennsylvania the summer before. He and Bill were both on the McKenzie ranch that winter, and they were lots of company for us. Some of the E6 boys would come up occasionally, and the north Cave Hills boys came to see us once in a while,

so we did not get very lonely. I went for the mail at Ashcroft pretty often.

We did not have much snow until in March. I think it
was about the tenth that it began to snow one afternoon and
kept it up all night. The next morning we had about a foot
of it, and as the wind had not blown, everything was covered
up. We had lots of hay, and as the grass could not be
reached, we thought we had better feed it until the snow
went off. A good many of the herd were way over on the
south side of the pasture. We saddled our horses and went
over after them. The sun was as bright as I ever saw it,
but it was not very cold. We got the cattle rounded up
and got about half way home with them when we both got
so snowblind we had to turn the cattle loose and try to get
home. Those who have never been snowblind cannot imagine
what we suffered while trying to get back to the ranch. One
suffering from snowblindness is not really blind, but his
face has been burned from the reflection of the sun on the
snow, and no human being can keep his eyes open at such
a time. The face feels just like it is scalded—and in fact it
has been, and the worst kind of a scald at that. Well, we
finally got home, went in the house, and shut out all the light
by putting blankets over the windows. When it was dark,
we found we could open our eyes, but we did not dare go
near a fire, or it would drive us wild. We had to wait until
dark to do our chores, and we had about one hundred head
of thin cows inside which had to be fed. I also had about
the same number of calves to look after, needing feed and
water. So after dark we hitched up a team and hauled feed,
and it was midnight by the time we got through. We were
both as hungry as wolves, but when we tried to cook a little,
without a light, it was like pouring boiling water over our
faces. We finally went to bed, but not to sleep. The next
morning the sun came up just as brightly as ever. We had
a black silk handkerchief apiece, so we doubled them, cut
holes for eyes, and tied them on our faces. That helped
some, but we were unable to have a light in the house for
about four nights. In about a week our faces peeled just

like they had been frozen. That was the only time I ever had that ailment, and I sincerely hope it will be the last.

The snow went off in a few days, and the grass began to peep up in places. We got along fine until March 28th, when it began to snow and blow and kept it up all night. We had turned our cows out in the pasture, and were feeding all that would come up at night. The wind and snow were so strong that it drifted the cattle to the southeast side of the pasture, and piled the snow up very badly. Next morning Jone said he would take a horse and see if he could pick a route by keeping on the higher ground, and we might get some of them back so we could feed them. He got back just as I had dinner ready and said the drifts were terrible. By leading his horse and keeping on the high ground, he did manage to get through.

He said, "That best registered Hereford cow just dropped a calf while I was over there, and we'll have to take a tarpaulin, wrap it up, and swing it on a pole between us and carry it home. It is a bull calf and worth a hundred and fifty dollars if we can save him."

He had taken the calf up before him, but the horse bucked so much he could not carry it, so he had wrapped it in his saddle blanket and buried it in a snowdrift.

After dinner we got the tarpaulin and a pole, and went after the calf. We broke as much of a road as we could as we went over empty, got over there, and dug Mr. Calf out. He had kept nice and warm in the snowbank. We wrapped him up and swung him to our pole and started. He did not seem heavy then, but the farther we went the deeper the snow seemed to get, and he was a load. In some places we wallowed through drifts four feet deep, but by resting quite often, we got home just at dark. That was the longest three miles I think I ever travelled. We always milked a cow or two, and they had not left the sheds, so we got some milk for our new pet and soon had him going fine, but the question was what to do with him during the night.

I said, "We will have to keep him in the house or he will freeze."

Jone said, "Yes, but you see he is very lively, and will be into everything in the house."

So I got a small rope and tied him to the bedpost, and after supper we fed him again and went to bed, but that calf could make more noise than a team of horses crossing a wooden bridge.

Next morning we took a scoop shovel and a team of horses and by shoveling through the drifts, we got some of the cattle home by mid-afternoon, and the calf's mother was in the bunch. The next day we got the rest of them home and that was the last snow of any consequence that spring. We sold the calf to Jim Hansen of the Slim Buttes that fall for $150.00, so I always thought we got well paid, in addition to the good exercise we got.

Grass started early that spring, and by the first of May we turned the cattle out of the pasture. Our range horses grazed about five miles southwest of the ranch on the divide between the head of Grand River and Jones Creek. They had wintered well. We had about ten head of three-year old geldings we wanted to break. Our horse corral was a big round one made with pitch-pine posts set six feet apart and sided up seven feet high almost solid with pine boards twelve feet long and twelve inches wide, with snubbing post in the center. One gate opened into the pasture and the other to the outside. We also had a small corral to one side in which we cut the horses that we wanted to take out of the main bunch. We ran them in and got out the ones we wanted to break, and always turned the main bunch out and let them go back to the range before we tried to take the others over to the ranch. We got along pretty well with the breaking. We had to do plenty of riding after the cattle while the grass was young and plenty of water everywhere, so that was a good way to break in young horses.

We had gotten word from home that father was not well that spring, so I thought I had better go down and see how things were going. I think it was about the middle of May I took a team down and was to bring some things back we needed. I went by Mr. Arpan's place on Indian Creek and hired Isaac to work for us that summer. When I got home, I found father in pretty bad health. He had been sick for about a month—not bedfast, but a long way from being well. He had been going to Deadwood every week to see the doctor, but said he did not seem to be getting any better. So I took out the things needed on the cowranch and came right back.

As they needed a team and two or three cows on the home ranch, I thought I would put out a few acres of corn to feed them. So I plowed about twenty five acres and planted corn, and to a fair sized garden already planted, I added some melons and potatoes. I took father to Belle Fourche once a week, where he took a train on to Deadwood. I stayed there and worked the corn until the middle of July, when father seemed to be better, and then took a load of supplies and a couple of hands back out to the hills to work in the hay.

When I got out there, I found the wolves had been working on our cattle, and had killed lots of calves and yearlings. Jone had Isaac herding through the day, so the cattle would be bunched at night, and Jone was night-herding, but still the wolves were getting a calf or yearling quite often. Jone said he had tried poison in every way he could think of but to no avail. We put the two men to haying, and Jone and I took a night about night-herding. I could always tell when wolves were around by the way the cattle would act. A shot or two would scare them away for awhile, but I have had them come two or three times in one night. We would scarcely ever see one in the day time. They always went back to the badlands on the head of Grand River and came out to do their killing after dark.

Jone was over on Jones Creek one day and found where they had killed a yearling that had been left out of the herd the night before. He thought he would look in some brush on the creek to see what he might find, and out jumped two Lobo wolves, as big as any collie dog, and just his luck to have no gun, but he was riding a mighty good horse, so he took down his rope and sailed in after them. They separated as soon as he started, and he said he picked the large one and caught up with him after about a quarter-mile run. On the first throw, Mr. Wolf jumped through the loop, but he had a horse he did not have to guide when roping anything, and he kept right after the wolf, and on the next throw, he necked him, then just swung his horse to one side and kept going, and he did not stop until the wolf was good and dead. He brought the hide and head home with him, and he was about as big a wolf as I have ever seen. Those big fellows are not hard to rope if you get them on smooth ground and they have just had a good feed. They certainly killed a lot of cattle for us through July and August of that year, with all of our night herding and care, in all, forty-two head. They may have killed more, but we found that many dead or crippled so badly they died later.

A strange thing about a wolf bite—if they caught a calf or yearling and tore the hold out and the animal got away, occasionally it would get well, but if they just sank their teeth in and did not tear it any, they died every time.

While dwelling on the subject of animal life in the wilds, I am reminded of an incident, which I believe occurred in June of that year, when brother Jone was with the E6 on the round-up and I was on the ranch alone. Joe Driscoll, the foreman, sent Tom Williams with about a half dozen boys to round up cattle on the heads of Jones and Bull Creeks. They came by the ranch, and as they were short-handed, I went with them. We looked through our cattle and took out all the range stock, and took them over on Bull Creek. We made a round-up there that evening and did not get through work until late in the day. As the boys had hardly enough help to hold the herd if it stormed, I stayed with them. Tom put me on first guard, and Bill Bankston said, as he came on second guard, for me to finish the night in his bed, as he had a double "tarp" and would not get wet if it rained (for it was thundering then). He put the bed on a little knoll, made by an old prairie dog hill, and told me where to find it when I came in.

The cattle were restless and hard to hold, as there was a bad looking cloud in the west with lots of thunder and lightning. It was coming slowly, but getting closer and worse looking all the time. About midnight, Tom told me to go in and send out the relief, and we would get to bed before it broke. Tom, Co Shirley, Hod Sikes, and Elmer Stambaugh were on first guard with me, and there were four to come on the second. We had just gotten in bed when the storm came, and I never saw it rain any harder. There was plenty of thunder and lightning, but no wind, fortunately, so the cattle were not hard to hold, but it rained as hard as it could until daylight, and everything was a flood. The creek was so high the night horse-wrangler had to swim it to get his horses to camp.

The boys had pulled their beds in under the cook and bed wagons, and when we began to crawl out to put our boots on, Elmer Stambaugh found a rattlesnake under the edge of his bed, Tom Williams found a bull snake in his, and by that time, old Lemy, the cook, found a big rattler under some wood he had put under the mess wagon to keep dry. The boys were all in for breakfast about then, and there was considerable excitement.

Hod Sikes, a big red haired Irishman, had rolled up his bed and was sitting on it, putting on his boots, laughing at the boys and having more fun than anybody, when all at once the most surprised expression came over that face of his I ever saw. He gave a whoop like an Indian on the warpath, tore out through the crowd of boys, like a dog with a tin-can tied to his tail, yelling "One in my boot! One in my boot!"

Some of the boys caught him, we jerked off a boot, and out fell one of those little prairie lizards (ground-puppies, we call them in Missouri) about three or four inches long.

Well, after we all laughed until we were almost sick, one of the boys asked Hood why he didn't pull off his boot, and he said he never thought of it.

When I was a boy, I used to read a piece in McGuffey's

Fourth Reader about King David who never smiled again after hearing of the death of his son Absalom. I know that if he had seen the expression on Hood's face as he flew around the camp, he would not only have smiled, but would have laughed out loud.

It was so muddy Tom said we would not hold the herd and not make a round-up that day.

I said, "One of my steers is in your herd, and if one of your boys will help me cut him out, I will take him home."

Tom said, "Did you see him last night?"

I said "No, but I heard him bawl."

Then you should have heard the boys laugh. So two or three of them went with me to see if I really had a steer in the herd. I told them a fellow was not much of a cow-man if he did not recognize the voices of his own cattle. I did not tell them that I never heard an animal with a voice just like that steer's.

The boys said, "No use trying to rustle any cattle off Virginia Bill, for he even knows their voices."

About the tenth of August, I received a letter from my brother-in-law, Dr. U. W. Showalter, that I was the father of a son born July 25th, weighing nine pounds, and named William Jackson, with mother and child doing nicely. The letter was written July 26th.

We were very busy those days trying to save our cattle from the wolves, and putting up hay. When we would find an animal fresh-killed, we would put all kinds of bait, with special scent, or anything we thought would draw them, around, but to no avail. The only ones we ever got were the few we shot or roped. To be sure, we were herding the main bunch of cattle, but there would always be a few that would be missed, and those were the ones they generally got.

I remember one night I was on guard, and it rained hard most of the night. The wolves came to the herd more than once that night, but I succeeded in scaring them away, and at daylight they had killed nothing. The cattle were just south of the pasture fence at the foot of South Mountain. It was very damp and cold, and I knew the day herder would be coming along soon, so I started home and met the herder less than two miles from the bunch, but when he got there, the wolves had come in and killed a calf, and two of them were eating on it. They were so busy, he got close before they saw the boy. He got one before they got to the foot of the mountain, where he could not follow. Evidently they had been watching me, and came down and made a kill as soon as I left.

We all talk about how smart and cunning dogs are, but they are far behind the cunning a wolf shows in killing stock and saving themselves from the lures and pitfalls man sets for them. I think we were more discouraged with the cattle business in the summer of '94 than at any time while we followed it, and I think we would have sold out cheaply, had a buyer come along.

One day, during the summer of '94, I was out looking after the stock, and on the ride I got over the divide on the north side of the mountain near George Dell's place. Mrs. Dell had not yet returned from Iowa. A few days before this, George was out after cattle and saw a big-horn doe and small kid crossing the valley and he gave chase, keeping them in smooth ground until he ran the kid down and caught it.

So this day I speak of, I met George, and after we talked a few minutes he said, "O Bill, I want you to come with me to the ranch, I have something I surely want you to see."

George had the best house in the hills. It had four log rooms in a string about 14 by 14 feet each, the first on the north being the kitchen, next the dining room, then the living room, with one bed in it, and the last was the guest room. The men slept in an outbuilding, known as the bunk-house, so when Mrs. Dell was not home, they did not use this bedroom. They had two beds in it, one under each window, and, as they did not use the room, George thought it would be an ideal place to keep the sheep.

We got to the house and George led the way through the living room, opened the door to the bedroom, and we both stepped inside. There was the little kid, about as big as a lamb two weeks old. It was the first I ever saw, so for a few moments I saw nothing but the kid, but directly I began to look at the surroundings, and I saw a trail of something that ran clear around the room and across both beds that looked something like thin plaster, but it was not plaster made of lime and cement. I called George's attention to it and he looked at it a bit, examined it more closely, and then what he said would not look well in print. That sheep had been running most of the time for two days in a circle around that room and had crossed under the windows and over the beds every time he made the trip. And the little fellow must have made many circles, judging from the trail he left.

Mrs. Dell had left her nicest quilts on the beds, so George was soon wondering how they would wash. I sure would have hated to have been in his shoes. It is now almost forty years since that happened, but I laugh yet everytime I think of it, and I suppose I will as long as I live.

As soon as my wife was able, she wrote me all about our son, and of course he was the most wonderful baby ever. It took a long time to exchange letters, and I was very impatient between messages.

Another little thing happened in the summer of '94 which gave me a right good joke on our neighbor, Bill Shaw.

The big cow outfits had been trying to ship out all their old Spanish (or Texas) bulls, and were replacing them with good Herefords, but there were a few which refused to leave their range, and when they would get on the fight and refused to go farther, the boys would just go on and leave them.

There was one such which ranged just below the Mc-Kenzie ranch. He belonged to the E6, but his Texas brand was a diamond with a tail to it. So we all called him "Old Diamond Tail."

One day Bill was up to our place and he said, "Old Diamond Tail has taken up with our herd and I can't get rid of him. I have run him off time and again, and the next day he is back. I ran him clear over on Grand River this morning, and if he comes back, I am going to kill him."

"Well," I said, "that is the proper thing to do, for he is the worst scrub I ever saw, and he can whip any good bull and run him clear away from the herd."

We had kept twenty of our best Hereford cows in the pasture and had our best Hereford bull with them. The next morning I was down in the pasture, and there was Old Diamond Tail with those cows, and our bull was gone. Diamond Tail had run him clear out of the pasture, and it riled me, so I just drove him about half a mile over on the creek and shot him.

So in a few days Bill was up again and he said, "Well, that last drive kept Old Diamond Tail away."

I said, "Well Bill, of course I know you killed him, but don't say anything about it for it might get you in trouble. Those big companies are funny that way."

"No, but honest Bill," he said, "I didn't kill him." And I said, "Of course, Bill, that is all right. I will never give you away, but I know what became of Diamond Tail."

And he tried many times to convince me he did not kill the bull, but I never did tell him how it was.

About the tenth of September, I went down to cut up my corn and found that father had not been so well, but was still able to be up. I had him try a new doctor who had come to Belle Fourche, and he appeared to get somewhat better. I got the corn cut up and was getting ready to go back out and help with the beef.

The night before I was to start, he and I were talking about the cattle we were to ship and about some we had bought from Charley Vansickle, when he looked at me in a queer way and began to talk in a language I could not understand. I saw by his looks that something serious was the matter. I asked what he meant, and he smiled and shook his head. I called my mother and sister and we put him in bed and I got my horse and went to Belle Fourche for the doctor, but when we got back, he was all right as far as his speech was concerned, but said his head hurt pretty badly. The doctor gave him something to ease the pain and said he thought he would be all right by morning. The next morning he said he felt much better and told me to go on to the ranch as I had planned, but I didn't go. I stayed over until the next morning, and as he was still feeling better, I decided to go on. He told me he knew what he wanted to say the night I went for the doctor, but could not form his speech into words.

I went on to the ranch. Jone had been alone, as Isaac Arpan had come down with me and was not going back until we shipped the beef.

Before I went down to cut the corn, we had bought Charlie Vansickle's cattle and ranch. We knew he had some good beef steers, but not quite enough for a load, and we thought we might buy them. We went to see Charlie and he said he would not sell the steers alone, but wanted to sell cattle and ranch. He had had some trouble with a cowboy who was working for George Dell, and he said the Cave Hills country was not big enough for the two of them. I tried to reason with Charlie and told him I did not believe the boy meant what he had said, and he said he was not afraid of what Shirley would do, but was uneasy about what he himself might do. So we bought him out. He was to stay and run the ranch until the next spring; we were to furnish him with meat and flour, and he to furnish all the rest of his grub. We gave him twenty dollars per head for all the cattle he counted to us and we got the brand and ranch. I do not remember the number he turned over to us, but I remember we got a few the next summer on round-up he had not counted to us.

After I got back to the ranch, we were busy fixing up sheds and getting wood, in addition to riding after the cattle. The wolves had not molested our stock lately.

On the last day of September, our cousin Will Hamilton came out after us, as father was much worse. He had started the night before, thinking he might get a change of horses at Macy, but failed to do so and had come on with the horses he started with. He got to the ranch just at dark. We had no horses in except the young ones we had been riding that day. All the rest had got the gate open and were out on the open range, and we knew it was useless to try to find them. So we started immediately with the two we had, hoping that Macy might have at least one horse in so one of us could go on anyway. We got to Macy at midnight, and as usual, not a horse was to be had. We fed ours, and let them rest about two hours, then Jone said he believed his horse could make it, and I said I would take mine as far as he could go. So we started on the next fifty mile lap. After the rest they went well for about twenty-five miles, and from that on they began to lag, and for the last two or three miles before we got to Fasberry's on Indian Creek, I walked and led my horse. Jone's horse seemed to be standing it better, but he was down to a slow walk. When I got to Fasberry's my horse could go no farther, and Mel had gone over to see how father was, and had ridden the only horse he had in. I left my horse, and as Jone's was still able to carry the saddle, we started on, Jone walking part of the time and I all the time. We kept together for a time, and then I went off and left them. I got home about nine o'clock that morning and Jone came in leading his horse about a half hour later. We found father better. He said he did not know they had sent for us and said he felt much better, so that they should not have alarmed us. Cousin Will said he would stay at the ranch and look after things until we got back.

The next morning I went to Belle Fourche and telephoned to Dr. Baker at Sundance, Wyoming to come and told him how father was. He got there about midnight, and as father was asleep (a thing which he did most of the time now) he said he would not go over him until morning. The next morning father had brightened up and appeared to be better, and Doc gave him a thorough examination, but he said there was very little hope for him, as he had an abscess of the brain. He turned to me and said, "If you think of any doctor you would like to try, have him come while I am here, so we can discuss the case together."

I said, "We have tried the best doctors of the Hills, and they have done him no good, so what is the use? I would rather risk your judgement than any of them."

He said that father might last a week or ten days, but the stuporous spells would get longer and come more often until the end; and that is the way it was, as on the tenth of October, our father passed away. About the same time, I received a letter from my wife telling of the death of her youngest brother, J. D. Showalter, of typhoid in Texas, so it was a very sad time for all of us.

After we had laid our father away, Jone went right back to the ranch, but I stayed a few days with mother and sister, and when I went, I took a young fellow out with me to cook for us as we brought the beef in.

The rest of the Cave Hills fellows had shipped from Dickinson while Jone and I were down below. With the beef we got from Vansickle, we had a nice herd of cows and steers, but the price was low and none of the Cave Hills men were satisfied with the returns. There were lots of complaints against Cleveland and his administration and about the low tariff on cattle, so we did not look forward to a bright future in the cow business.

We got our cattle gathered to go south with them and Isaac Arpan came out to stay at the ranch while we were gone, and then planned to stay with Jone on through the winter.

In the spring, when Jone and I were breaking horses,

we had a young horse which got crippled when a yearling, and we kept him with the saddle horses so we could doctor him. By the time he was well, he had become so tame he was a pet, and we just let him stay with the saddlers after that. He was four years old now, and was a fine specimen of horseflesh, about fifteen hands high and would weigh near eleven hundred pounds.

So Jone said one afternoon, "Let's ride the pet."

We walked up to him, put his bridle on, saddled him, and led him around a little, then Jone got on. We then rode down to see the Shaw boys, and when we came back in the evening, turned him with the rest of the saddle horses. No one could tell but that he was a well-broke horse.

In about a week after that, one Sunday while Jone was out after the cattle, I said to Ike, "Let's go over to Dell's." I got the "Pet," as we called him, and we went up the near way over the mountain and just after we got down in the valley, on the other side, that horse went up in the air, got his head down between his front legs, and bawled life a calf; and I never got such a pounding in my life. Just as I thought I was gone, he stopped still, and I eased back in the saddle and pulled his head up, got hold of my quirt, and fanned him for about a hundred yards, and he was all right. But when I went to start home, he went after me again and it was all I could do to stay with him. We told Jone about it that night and he had a good laugh at me and said it was the way I handled him, that he would not buck with him.

The next morning we were going up the creek about four miles to cut some ash poles we needed, and he said if I would carry the axes, he would ride the bad horse. So we pulled out and the horse went fine and never made a bobble, and Jone laughed more than ever. We cut all the poles we needed, got our horses to start home, and just as Jone lit in the saddle, the pet went after him, and with a downhill swing, I thought for awhile he would sure get him. Finally the quirt got too hot for him, and he threw up his head and started for home. When I got down to the ranch, Jone had turned the horse out and was standing looking at him.

I said, "What do you think of him?"

"Well," he said, "he is not the hardest horse to ride I ever rode, but he is the hardest bucker."

And we both rode him several times that summer, but I do not remember that he was ever ridden after that he did not buck sometime before we got off him.

When we got everything ready, and started, it was late in October, and the nights were getting pretty cold. Willis and Will Hamilton, our cousins, Fred Croshane, Jone and I constituted the crew. Fred was the cook, and he led two horses we used for night herding. We drove to Belle Fourche, and because of the coolness of the weather, we made the trip in eight days. The weather was dry, and the days fine, but it got pretty chilly on herd of nights. Of evenings we would gather lots of buffalo or cow-chips, and keep a big fire all night, so when we came in off guard we could get warm before going to bed. I thought I would break that sorrel horse, so I rode him every day on the trip, but there was not a day he didn't take a try at me sometime. I will have something to say about this horse later on.

We got down all right, and Jone went with the shipment to Chicago. I got wood for the winter while he was gone. We only got $3.50 for our best that fall, and $2.00 for good fat cows.

When Jone got back, we settled up the estate. We bought mother and sister out, and we deeded our interest in the homestead to mother, and after it was all settled up, mother and sister went back to W. Va. for the winter. As my wife was wanting to come home, it was agreed we should live on the homestead while they were away. Jone went back to the ranch and Isaac stayed with him through the winter.

About the middle of November, mother and sister went East, and the last of the month, my wife and boy came home.

The boy was now four months old, and I had not seen him before. I had everything ready for winter, and as I only had three cows and three horses to care for, I had a pretty easy season. I got up some more wood and husked out what corn I had that Jackrabbits had not eaten. I did not hear from Jone but once or twice that winter.

We had no school at our school house, as the families had all moved away with nothing left but the bachelors.

We had to fall on some plan for getting rid of the wolves on the ranch or go out of the stock business, so we decided to try dogs. We got some stag and grey hounds, and I wrote to an uncle in W. Va. to have him get us four fox or trail hounds. He sent us four of the best he could find, two male, two female, the kind that never quit a trail. I do not remember what he paid, but he said they were the best the mountains afforded. I do remember that their express to Belle Fourche was $75.00, but we never regretted the expense.

The trail hounds were scarcely ever in on the kill, but had it not been for them, we could not have got them out of the badlands and brakes. The stag and grey hounds did the catching and killing, but were no good at trailing. Jone and the Hamilton boys took the two staghounds and three greyhounds out in the fall of '94. The foxhounds I kept on the river ranch until spring.

There was one great trouble about trying to keep dogs at the ranch—we had put out poison for wolves, lots of it in small pieces of meat, and in that dry climate it would just dry up, and would kill a dog if he picked it up years afterwards. One of the greyhounds got poisoned as Jone took him out to the ranch, getting the poison after he got inside our pasture. And another great trouble was porcupines—it was terrible to have a bunch of dogs run on to a porcupine. Those quills came out of "porky" very easily, but when we went to pull them out of a dog's mouth, it was another matter. We used pliers for that purpose.

In the spring I got a letter from Jone asking me to

send him a man to help him break a few horses, as Isaac was too light for the work. He said he had already hired a pretty good man to take the Vansickle ranch at Table Mountain, by the name of Ed Labree. I hired Bill Maine. I told him I wanted a man to help break some horses in the spring and stay on through the summer, that he would be expected to ride horse about with Jone. It was agreed that we give him $35.00 per month and board for the summer. He had two horses, so he packed his bed on one and rode the other and went out about the middle of April. I told him his wages started the morning he left for the ranch.

He went out in two days and he and Jone fixed up the corral and got ready to begin. They went out on the range and ran the bunch in, then cut out seven of the best looking ones. They were fine horses, pretty big for cow-horses but the kind that could carry a man all day.

After they got the bunch with the balance of the saddle horses, Jone said: "Bill, that sorrel there was a pretty hard horse to ride last summer, and we never did get him broke from bucking. As I understand his gait, I will take him and you take the first green horse."

So they drove the bunch, old and green, in the small corral at the ranch, and Jone walked up to Pet and put his bridle on him.

Bill said, "Jone, let me have him for my first horse."

Jone said, "Well, all right, but I will tell you, he is hard to ride."

Bill said, "You rode him didn't you?"

"Yes, but I know his gait."

"Well, if you can ride him, so can I."

Jone said, "All right, put your hull on him."

So he saddled him and got on him, and the horse walked around like any gentle horse would, and Bill had a big laugh.

Jone said, "When I open the gate, be ready."

Bill answered, "I am always ready to ride such horses as this."

He was at the opposite side of the corral when Jone opened the gate, and here he came—and just as he went out the gate, the sorrel went after him, and on the third buck, Bill went over his head.

He jumped up and said, "Snub him to your saddle horn and I will ride him."

"No," Jone said, "you can't ride him one jump that way. The only way to stay on that horse is to ride him straight up and give him the quirt."

But to satisfy Bill, Jone did snub him to his saddle horn. Bill got on, they went about fifty yards, and Pet thought that was far enough, so he gave one terrible plunge forward, and being tied to the horn, giving him such a sudden stop with his head low and his hind parts high in the air, Bill shot right off and again stood on his head.

He jumped up and said, "I can't ride those d—— big horses. You will have to get someone else."

Jone said, "I told you I would ride this horse, you pick the first green horse."

"Oh just look at those big devils," Bill groaned. "I know they will just kill a man."

"There may not be a one of them buck," Jone said. "They are not usually hard to ride."

But Bill would not stay, or take any pay for the work he had done. So the next morning he pulled down to the E6 ranch.

There were lots of boys there wanting jobs. Bill was telling of his experiences at the Hamilton ranch and one fellow asked if the Hamiltons still wanted a man. Bill says "Yes, they do, but you don't think you could ride those horses do you? Why man, they are as big as elephants and are regular man-killers!" The boy said he wanted a job and would try most anything.

The boy came up that same evening, and that night he told Jone what Bill had said and asked for a job. Jone said he would see about it in the morning.

He was a French boy, by the name of Louis Canoy. Next morning Jone said to Louie, "I have a horse here. If you can ride him and not pull leather, I will give you $35.00 per month to help me break seven horses and stay with us the rest of the summer."

Lou said, "I will try."

So they ran the horses in and caught the pet. Jone said the boy's outfit looked mighty common, and he told him he could use his oufit if he liked.

He said "No, I would have to take up the stirrups. I will try my own old hull. But is he hard to get on?"

"No," Jone said, "he will not move until you are in the saddle, but then he moves pretty fast."

He got on him in the corral and after he rode around a time or two he said, "Open the gate," and away he went. And just as he went out the gate, he went at it. Jone said Lou had his quirt in his hand and he sat on that horse and fanned him on both sides from his head to his tail, and took him around a little through the pasture and back. And when he came back, Jone said, "You will do. And you may have that horse to ride when and where you please all summer."

I think Lou was the slickest rider I ever saw, but was very slow to get on. I told him once if I could sit in the saddle like he did, I could ride any horse that wore hair, for I had never found a horse I could not get on. My great trouble was staying in the saddle.

I put out some wheat, oats and corn that spring, as my wife and I did not think we could go to the ranch that summer. Mother and sister were still in W. Va. and would not be back until fall. After I got my crop in, I went to the ranch to take supplies and the foxhounds. Jone wrote that he was having considerable sport with the four dogs he had.

One had died from poison. He had killed only two wolves, but had taken lots of coyotes.

It was rather amusing about the coyotes. When we first took the dogs out to the ranch, and they started after a coyote, he would stand and look at them until they got up close, then he would start with all his might, but very seldom got away. But after the dogs had been to the ranch for awhile, when we saw a coyote, he was running and he kept it up until he either got caught or made his getaway.

About the first of June I went out. I got a woman and her little boy to stay with my wife and baby while I was gone. The next day after I got there, Jone said he knew where two wolves stayed over in the brakes at the head of Grand River, but the greyhounds could do nothing with them. The ground was too rough.

So the next day we took the eight dogs and went over about five miles, and it was not an hour after we got to the rough ground until one of the trail hounds struck a warm trail, the other three joined in, and my, that was fine music! But the greyhounds did not know what to make of it and would not join in, but stayed with us.

I said, "We will keep the greyhounds with us, and keep on the high ground. In that way we may get sight of Mr. Wolf."

We had not been up on the ridge twenty minutes until a wolf came up out of the badlands with all four of the trailers not more than two hundred yards behind him. As soon as the greyhounds saw him, they needed no encouragement to go. They all made for him, and we cut in between him and the brakes to keep him in the smooth country. They caught him before he had gone a quarter of a mile, and although we got there almost as soon as the hounds, they had the wolf almost dead before the trail hounds came up; but they ran in and grabbed that wolf just like they had done the whole thing. We were certainly well pleased with the way those trailers worked, and you may be sure that money could hardly have bought them.

This was a dog wolf and we knew that his mate and whelps were in there somewhere.

Jone told me he was going down to be married before hay-making time. As the corn needed plowing, I went back to the river until hay season, when I planned going up to help the man at Table Mountain.

Jone came down soon after and was married to Miss Armein Arpan. Her parents lived on Indian Creek and were Canadian born of French descent. She had been raised on the frontier and was used to it, and in a few days they went out to the ranch to live.

I plowed my corn over a couple of times, and as it was too dry for the small grain to fill, I cut it for hay, and then went out to help make hay at Table Mountain. I got Mrs. Roberts to stay with the wife and boy and went out about the middle of July. Jone had hired another man and was making hay when I got out there. I took a new machine to be used at the Table Mountain ranch, and Ed Labree and I went at it.

I shifted the cooking on Ed and I did the milking and cared for the teams. This worked out fine. Hay was much better up there than it was at the home ranch, and we got it up almost as fast as the three men did at the old place.

But I think they put in considerable time chasing wolves. We had lost another greyhound by poison, but still had the four old foxhounds and eight young ones coming on. I took out several hundred pounds of corn meal with me, and Jone's wife made bread for them. We fed them meat in winter. Jone had quite a time with porcupines. One greyhound was rather cross anytime, and when he got a dose of quills, he was mean.

Ed and I were pretty busy and did not have time to lose running range cattle, and they were thick up there. So one morning I said I was going to get rid of them.

Ed said, "I have tried everything I know of, but they come right back."

"I have a plan that never fails," I said, "but we must keep it to ourselves."

So we both went out and rounded our back toward the ranch and moved the range cattle quietly over the divide toward the Little Missouri. Then we rode back over the divide out of sight and I told Ed to keep the horses and wait for me. I went back on foot, and as soon as I came in sight, the cattle all stuck up their heads and started towards me. I kept walking slowly toward them, took off my hat, and moved it up and down in front of my face, far enough so I could see the cattle above and under the hat, and kept going toward them all the time. They ran toward me until they were about one hundred yards away, and then turned and ran about a hundred, then whirled around and stopped facing me. I kept right on toward them. Once more they wheeled and started, and I know they never stopped until they crossed the river ten miles away, and every bunch that saw them running joined in with them. We were bothered no more in a month.

That trick will work on old gentle milk cows. If you don't believe it, try it sometime when they are out on pasture.

While Jone was down on the river the first of July we heard that the Armstrong Brothers, over in Montana about forty miles west of us, had fifty steers they wanted to sell. They were three and four years old. I told Jone to go look at them when he got back to the ranch, and if they priced them right and would count them to us at shipping time that fall, to buy them. He did and bought them at $30.00 per head. They were mostly grade Hereford, and while he was over there he bought the Burdett Bros.' herd, as fine a little herd of pureblood Herefords as I have ever seen. It was only fifty head in all.

After Ed and I got rid of the range cattle, we got along with the hay faster and I went back to the river the last of August. We were going to ship from Belle Fourche that year.

It had been so dry down on the river my corn had not made much, and it was ready to cut up by the first of September.

I was to bring some money out with me to buy some steers from the settlers in the Long Pine Hills. They would have from four or five to a dozen head apiece, and they had always shipped with the Armstrong boys, but as they had sold at home, the others wanted to sell, and they all wanted cash, not checks. I was to go out horseback. The wife and boy had gotten along fine while I was away, but I had to be away so much, he hardly knew I belonged there.

I went to the bank and got $3500.00 with which to buy cattle. A neighbor had a good young horse he wanted me to ride on the trip out and back. When we came with the beef he said he was broke, but not as gentle as he wanted him. I took him and started, noticing that he was a little headstrong when I first got on him. I put most of my money in my coat pockets and rolled it inside my slicker, then tied it on behind my saddle.

When I was out on Two-top Divide, my blanket had worked back and I thought I would fix it. I got off, and before I loosened the cinches, he jerked away from me, and away he went, right straight north.

"Now," I said, "I am a-foot twenty-five miles from nowhere, and three thousand dollars tied in that slicker."

I had a spade bit on my bridle, and I always rode with open reins, so when the horse stopped running, he began to step on the reins and the bit cut his mouth so badly he stopped and turned head to me, and I eased up and caught him. The first thing I did was to take that slicker off the saddle, and I put the coat on, even if the weather was hot.

The dogs caught a good many wolves that summer. Jone and Lou got the mate to the one I helped catch, and found the den and got six pups. That saved us enough cattle to pay all the trail hounds cost us.

We had one English greyhound that was different from

any other greyhound I ever saw. He was a very large dog, weighing almost one hundred pounds. Greyhounds usually snap and cut, but this dog caught by the throat and kept his hold like a bull-dog, and nothing could shake him loose. I have seen him stand and watch the other dogs fight until he saw an opening for the throat, then grab it and lie down until the wolf was dead. We gave $25.00 for this dog and it was a fine investment. He was not nearly as fast as the other greyhounds. We had one small dark blue hound which always did the catching—he was very swift, but was not much for a fight, but kept him engaged until the others got there, and when the others got him stretched out, then he would tear a hole in the flank before you could wink.

We lost but very few cattle that first summer after we got the dogs. The best wolf hounds we got were the cross between the grey and the foxhounds. They got good sized, were fast enough, and fast trailers, running a trail almost as fast as by sight, and were the greatest fighters I ever saw. They simply would not give up. They would do lots of howling while in a fight, but fought all the harder. The dogs saved us plenty of cattle and colts, and gave us lots of sport. Our horses got so we could scarcely hold them when we jumped a wolf. We never allowed the dogs to run antelope if we could help it. We did not want them chased, and I don't believe a greyhound ever lived fast enough to catch one anyway. At least we did not have one.

We only had one hound which could catch a jackrabbit, and he was not the swiftest either. I noticed that the rabbit was always up in the air when the dog caught it. I began to wonder at this, and watched him closely. He first threw them up with his nose, and grabbed them before they hit the ground. I do not know the philosophy for this, but never-the-less, it is true.

When I got back to the ranch, the boys were about done haying, so in a few days we were ready to go over to the Long Pine Hills after the cattle we had bought. We rigged up a mess wagon and took a tent. Cousin Will Hamilton, Isaac Arpan, Fred Sutton, Jone, his wife, and myself made the party. Lou stayed behind and held down the ranch while we were gone. Jone's wife said she wanted to drive the mess wagon and do the cooking. We went over in one day. The next day Jone and I scouted around in the hills and bought some good beef, the parties all to deliver them at Armstrong Bros. on a certain day. While we were at this, our boys were helping the Armstrongs round up their cattle.

We went over to see the Burdett boys and they said they would bring their cattle to Armstrong's ranch the day we were to start home. Everything worked out according to schedule, and we started just afternoon with the herd, aiming to get down to the Missouri River bottom to camp for the night. Two of the Armstrong boys said they would help us that afternoon and stay with us the first night, as it would be a tough job to hold that bunch of ranch cattle that close home. Jone went on with his wife to find a suitable camping place and we followed. The weather was fine, and by having plenty of help, we got along well. Jone had everything ready, his wife had a good meal served when we got there, and we grazed the cattle out on the river bottom while we went to supper by twos. We put two on guard at a time at two hours each, and as there were eight of us, we only stood guard the one shift. The next morning Will, Gene Armstrong, and Bud Burdett helped us across the river, and then went back home. Counting the stock cattle and beef, we had about two hundred head, and it made a nice bunch to handle. So many different bunches were represented, that they had to be watched very closely, as ranch cattle are much harder to handle than range herds.

We crossed the river near Ashcroft and had good grass all the way, camping for noon in a small creek where we could get water, as we knew we would have to make a dry camp that night on the divide between the river and the head of Jones Creek. We hauled a keg of water to cook with that night and the next morning. The cattle behaved well that night, and next day we got home by noon and turned them into the pasture. The next day we went up to the Table Mountain ranch and rounded up the bunch, cut the beef out, and kept them in the corral that night so we did not have to stand guard. The boys all went back to the Jones Creek ranch that night so they could round up our beef by the time Ed and I got down to the ranch the next afternoon. We got all the beef in the pasture that night and rounded them all up near the ranch, where we stood guard through the night so we could start south with them the next morning. Willis and Will Hamilton were going down with us. Lou, Fred, Jone and his wife, and I constituted the crew. The weather was fine, grass good, and we were only aiming to make about ten miles per day. Water was a little scarce and we sometimes had to drive off the trail to find enough for the stock. We got two or three steers mired in the mud at some of the watering places, having to use our ropes several times; but we were fortunate enough to have horses that pulled well by the saddle horn. Sometimes we had to put two or three horses on a steer.

We got down near the settlement, and I went on home one night to see how Mrs. H. and the boy were getting along. I had been gone more than two weeks and had heard nothing from them in that time. I found out while down there that the price of beef was very low, and Uncle Will had a pasture on his claim across the river which had not been grazed so he said he would rent it to us if we wanted to put our beef on it for awhile. I rented it and went back to meet the herd at Indian Creek, and instead of going on to Belle Fourche, we drove them straight south to the pasture.

We had left Isaac at the ranch to look after the stock. We held the cattle two weeks, when the price got a little better, but if the cattle had not gained, it would not have paid the extra expense. About the 20th of October we shipped them from St. Onge. They weighed well, but we got only $3.50 for the best and $3.25 for the balance, with cows at $2.00. At that, we made some money on the cattle we bought.

Jone and Minnie went back to the ranch for the winter, and Isaac stayed on with them. Mother and sister came back in October, so I rented a house and barn near my ranch, and we moved there in November. It was close by and I moved my feed and got up wood for the winter.

My sister married William Dolan, a neighbor boy, and they made their home with mother that winter. I was now living near my Uncle Will's and we were quite a lot of company for each other. Alden's wife and little girl lived with them. Alden was out on the cow ranch. He and Uncle Will had moved about eight miles farther north of our ranch on North Grand River in North Dakota, and they had bought Willis and Will out.

Jone took plenty of corn meal with his winter supplies to give the dogs a change from beef occasionally. We had several young dogs coming on now. It always was strange to me that wolves never bothered our cattle during winter. We always lost the most in July and August and a few in September. We had a pretty hard winter and the range men lost heavily. Jone had plenty of hay at the home ranch and so did Ed at Table Mountain.

On April 3, 1896, our second child was born, and we named her Sarah Lucretia after her two grandmothers. I did not go out to the cow-ranch until the last of May. We kept a girl now to do the house work and be company for my wife.

On my way out to the ranch to take supplies, I got caught and had to lay over two days just north of Two-top divide. There were about thirty miles of the worst gumbo I ever saw between Indian Creek and Macy, and when it rained on a fellow in there, there was nothing to do but stop until it dried.

I wanted to rent a house in town and have my wife live there while I stayed with the cattle, but she said no, if I were going to stay on the ranch, she would also. So we began to make arrangements to move out. While I was out in June, Isaac and I took two teams and went over in the Long Pine Hills in Montana to a sawmill and got enough lumber to build a two room house, and before I went back south, we got the house sided up and a roof on so we would have shelter. I had rented my corn land out to a neighbor, and he took in what I had put out, so I had nothing to detain me on the river. We got under way and got out to the ranch in July. Jone came in with another team to get his wife. She had gone down to her parents on Indian Creek early in the spring, and their first child, a boy, was born in June.

After we got each family in its own house, we were pretty well satisfied. Our houses were only about two hundred yards apart, so the women folks could visit with one another. Isaac still worked for us, and by hay time, we hired Hope Slaughter to help out.

I had not had any sport with the dogs for sometime. Jone was going to the Table Mountain ranch one day while Ike and I were after lumber. He did not aim to take any of the dogs, but two greyhounds and three of the half-blood young dogs followed him, and just as he crossed Bull Creek, they ran a wolf out of the brush and caught him near a big water hole, and in the course of the fight, he got into the water. Jone said he did not dare shoot, in fear of hitting a dog, but he said that wolf was about to drown the lot of the dogs. He would put them under as fast as they came to him. Jone got his rope, and when they came near the bank, he threw it on the wolf and drew him to the bank, where the dogs soon killed him. Jone said that was the largest wolf he ever saw. He brought the hide and head home and it measured nine inches from the tip of the nose to the top of the head.

One day after we had gotten moved, Jone and I went down in the pasture looking after a bunch of Hereford cows and calves, with some of our dogs along, and they started a wolf. He ran over to South Mountain, and crawled in between two rocks that lay one on top of the other. There was only one place where he could get in, but we could see him from two or three places. I cut a long slim pole and got to punching him from the opposite side, and when his attention was on me, two of the dogs got a hold on him and pulled him out. Jone held the old big greyhound and just let the five half-breed young dogs have him. I never saw such a fight. Those young dogs would squall like the wolf was killing them, but they never quit until he was a dead wolf.

One day not long after this happened, Jone and I were going down to the McKenzie ranch, and about two miles from the ranch house we looked up at the foot of the rimrock and saw five mountain sheep. One was a buck with the largest horns I ever saw. We had nothing but six shooters and we could get no closer from the south side of the mountain, so we went back to the house and left our horses. Jone got his Winchester and I a shotgun loaded with buckshot and we went up through a cut to the top, then went out to where the sheep would be just under us. We found a crevice in the cliff. I was to run out on the edge as soon as I heard him shoot, and with the buckshot, I was sure I could get two. When he shot, I ran out, and right under me about one hundred yards distant stood the big buck with horns that looked as big as stove pipes. I pulled both barrels, and it looked as though I tore a hole in the ground as big as a gallon bucket on either side of that sheep, but I never touched him, and Jone only got a small doe. He said the buck had kept out of his sight behind a rock. Once before this I had a fair shot at a sheep but did not get it. I could kill deer and antelope, but apparently mountain sheep were not for me.

A few days after this we were out for a wolf chase and had all the dogs with us except three or four pups that were too young for training. Mrs. Hamilton said she heard the pups making considerable noise and she went to the door. There in the yard was a big wolf playing with them. She got her six-shooter and stepped outside the door, but was afraid to shoot until he got some distance away as the pups were between her and the wolf. When she got a chance, she let him have it. She told us about it when we came in and I asked her where her wolf was.

She said, "I did not kill him, but I crippled him."

I laughed and said, "You just scared him."

She told me which way he went, out over a small butte nearby. Next day I rode out that way to look after some cows, and sure enough, I found a dead wolf that had been shot through the body.

That fall quite a bunch of Indians came up in the Cave Hills hunting and gathering plums—about thirteen wagons of them. Their chief was Little-Man-Afraid-of-his-Horse. This was the first time they had been up in there since Sitting Bull was killed. They would come to the house, and after wanting to trade meat for groceries, they would steal all they could find, unless one kept an eye peeled.

That fall I was getting rock from a little butte near the house to wall a well, and I ran onto a den of rattlesnakes. We killed twenty-five in one day. They always come back to the mountains to winter.

One day that fall the dogs came on to a porcupine and five or six got a terrible dose of quills. We had quite a job pulling them out. Some of the dogs were hard to manage, for they would fight. We lost one of our old fox-hounds. She got so many quills, and in so deep, we could not get them out.

There were some changes made in our settlement the summer of '96. George Dell sold his ranch and stock to Gus Schleighardt, a miner from Lead City. Gus was a good fellow and we all liked him, but he knew nothing about stock. However, he was willing and anxious to learn.

We sold our Table Mountain ranch and fifty head of cattle to Albert Clarkson for $1500.00. We had more cattle now and it was harder to get hay outside the pasture. We did not want to cut hay inside, as we needed it for grazing, so we decided to go up on top of the mountain. It was three miles west to where we could get a team up on top, and too steep to haul a load down, while it was only about two hundred yards from the foot of the cliff to our sheds. We hauled the hay and pitched it over the cliff, and it would slide to the level below. Then we would load it on a wagon and haul it to the corral. To be sure, we had to load it twice, but that was much faster than hauling five or six miles. We could take our teams up singly through the cut in the cliff. Hay was good on top of the mountain, as the cattle never grazed up there.

We had lots of dogs now, counting all ages. We did not kill many wolves, but the dogs kept them scared out pretty well. If we could hear them howl out on the range at night, we were never too busy to take the dogs out in that vicinity next morning, and we would most always have a chase with scarcely ever one getting away. Our horses were as anxious for the chase as the hounds. It cost us considerable to feed the dogs, but not nearly so much as to feed the wolves. Our wives took turns at baking bread for them. They had a breadpan each that was the size of the stove oven, and they cut the bread in squares to dole it out. It was amusing to see them at feeding time, the dogs sitting in a circle around my wife while she threw each dog a square, which he always caught and then waited for his next turn.

One of the greyhounds got bit by a rattlesnake many times. The first time, I was sure he would die. His head swelled so badly he could not chew or swallow for several days, and during that time spent all his time lying in the mud down at the creek. He was the only dog we had which would grab a snake while it was coiled. We had others that would kill snakes, but they would always wait until the snake started to crawl, and then grab it and shake it to pieces. I think this dog got immune to snake venom, for he got so it affected him very little when bitten.

I have not said how we branded our stock. We used the Bow-and-Arrow for Cattle and ER for horses. We always had a kind of frolic on branding day; all the neighbors would come and help. We would brand one place one day and another the next until all the neighbors were done.

We all shipped together the fall of '96, and as the feed was better to the north, we went to Dickinson. Jone was going with the cattle. We gathered ours and drove to Bull

Creek, and there Schleighardt, Johnson and Connell joined us with theirs. We drove north to the west side of the Cave Hills for dinner. After dinner Gus thought he would change horses. He had a little bay horse he got from Dell and he had not been ridden for some time. He usually bucked a little after running idle for a while. Gus saddled him and got on without moving him, and he just stood still and did not want to move.

Gus says, "Boys, what's the matter with him?"

I said, "Stick your spurs to him and he will move."

And he did. He moved so fast that after about three jumps, Gus sat flat on the ground in front of him. Some of the boys caught the horse and brought him back, Gus got on again, and he went all right. I told Gus if he had moved him a little before getting on, he would not have bucked and he said he sure would move him next time.

All the Hills fellows joined us that afternoon and we camped near where we were for dinner, having a nice smooth place to bed the cattle, but it was not far from the badlands. I stayed with them that night, as we always needed more help then.

On second guard, Gene Johnson, Will Hamilton, Gus, and I were on duty, and the cattle were all quiet and nearly all bedded down. Gus and I were on one side and Will and Gene on the other. I rode up to Gus and said it must be near midnight. He took out his watch, and as it was pretty dark scratched one of those old popping matches to have a look, and at that two or three steers jumped up. That started some more, giving them a worse scare, and before you could think, they were in a general stampede. I told Gus to follow me and we pulled in between the herd and the badlands to keep them on smooth ground, but about one-third broke by us into the rough country and all we could do was to let them go and keep the others in a circle until we got them quiet. Had we not been so near the badlands, we might have held them. Some of almost everyone's cattle got away and it took almost two days to get them back and get started. Gus said, "I wonder what started them?"

Gus got into lots of trouble before he learned to be a full-fledged rancher. He told me about the first saddle horse he tried to break. He said he got him in a stable and tied him up in a stall, and at first he tied a curry comb on a short stick, long enough so the horse could not kick him until the horse got pretty well used to it, then saddled him, keeping the stall between him and the horse. He said he did not buck with the saddle and seemed so gentle he thought he would get on him while he was tied to the stall. The loft floor over the stall was of pine poles and was not laid close up together, the loft being empty of hay at the time. So Gus eased himself into the saddle and everything went lovely for a minute or two, until the horse went to bucking, and he said every time the horse went up, his head went up between the round poles. He said he didn't mind going up so much as the coming down for it almost pulled his ears off on the down trip. He said "When that horse got quiet I got off, and believe me I ride no more broncs in a stable."

And he told me many more funny things I have forgotten.

We had only three carloads of steers in the fall of '96. Jone went out to a Hereford breeder near Chicago and bought a carload of young Hereford bulls for ourselves and the rest of the Cave Hills neighbors. When he got back to Dickinson, Gene Johnson, Will McVeigh, Fred Curliss and Will Hamilton, who had gone to Chicago with the shipment, also helped bring the bulls on to the Hills. They had left their team at Dickinson. The rest had come back horseback after the cattle had been loaded.

After they got home, we turned the cattle into the pasture and fixed the sheds, then got up wood for the winter. We got Albert Clarkson to bring some supplies for us when he got his. It was getting pretty late and we did not want to be away from home. Al got caught in a blizzard the last day on his return but he had a team which had been over the road several times and that helped. He said he could not see the road at times and would stop the team and hunt for it, then start on. He managed to get inside the pasture about ten that night and had to leave his load and lead his team on in. It took him almost two hours to make the last three miles. We kept a light burning in the window for him but he said he did not see it until he was within fifty yards of the house. We took four horses and went after the load the next day and had to shovel through many drifts.

Jim Hansen and Charlie Calbic came over from the Slim Buttes that winter to buy some bulls and Jim stayed with me, Charlie with Jone. Jim was a great fellow to smoke a pipe, and that night we were all sitting around the stove and Jim had his pipe going full blast. My wife missed our little three year old boy and she went back to the bedroom, where she found him under one of the beds. She said, "Jack, what is the matter with you, what did you come in here in the cold for?"

He said, "Oh, I'm afraid that man will blow up. Don't you see how the smoke comes out of his mouth?"

He was not used to seeing anyone smoke, as Jone nor I neither used tobacco and we would never hire a man who smoked, because there was so much danger of prairie fire, And I did not care to be smoked up anyway.

Mrs. Phil Bonniwell came over from the Slim Buttes that fall and visited with our wives for about ten days and they were mighty glad to have her. That was the only woman they saw from July until the next June.

We had some nice weather after the November storm was over, with no severe weather until after Christmas. It set in the first of January and for sixteen days it never got warmer than sixteen below zero, with a strong northwest wind every day and clear most of the time. The wind would go down as the sun did and come up at sunrise. The cattle did all their grazing from sundown until about midnight. Fortunately, there was very little snow.

We were not bothered with wolves during the cold spell, but about the 20th of January they began to howl around pretty close and we got out with the dogs and caught a few, but it was not much sport while the ground was frozen, as our horses would get very much excited. It was almost impossible to hold them when the dogs got started, and we both got some pretty hard falls.

I remember one chase which took place Feb. 2, '97. The wolves had been howling almost all night, and the next morning they were getting 'most too bold. We thought we had better go over on the flat and give them a scare anyway. I said I did not like the idea very much, as the snow had thawed with a chinook wind a few days before and had frozen suddenly, making considerable ice, especially where the grass was pretty heavy, and a rider could not see it until he struck it. We only kept two saddle horses up during winter and one of them no man could hold when those dogs started anything. So I made it a point to get to the stable first and put my saddle on the other horse. Jone always was a little more reckless on frozen ground than I was anyway. So we got ready and called the whole pack, and they were very anxious to go, as they had not been out for sometime. We had about fifteen full grown dogs of different kinds, and when they all got under way, it made quite a commotion. We got over in the neighborhood of where we heard the wolves the night before, the dogs got their noses in the air and started toward the northwest, facing the wind, and when they started, so did we. It was about a half a mile to the top of the next divide, and we could not see what we were after until we got to the top. The dogs went over the top with us not far behind, and just as we came to the top, I looked a short distance ahead of the dogs. There was an old buck antelope, and he was going some, with the fifteen dogs strung out after him. I began to pull my horse in, but I knew Jone had just as well push on the reins, as to pull for his horse would have to fall or run himself down before he could stop him. The grass was pretty heavy, and he was running on a slope where water had frozen, and I stopped and almost held my breath; and directly I saw him fall while running at full speed. I saw the horse get up and stand still, but Jone did not rise. I went as fast as I could, and when I got there, Jone was sitting up, and I asked him if he was hurt.

He said, "I think not seriously, but it knocked the wind all out of me."

When the horse started to fall, he pulled his feet out of the stirrups and landed on his hands and knees, horse and all sliding a good fourteen paces, cutting that grass as smooth as if it had been gone over with a lawn mower. Jone had no knees left in his pants, or skin on his knees, and his gauntlet gloves were all torn on the palms. When the horses stopped, the dogs soon stopped also, as we never allowed them to run anything but wolves and rabbits. Jone was pretty stiff for several days, and we did not try any more chases until the ground got good and dry.

In February, our little boy got sick and had us all greatly worried. We had plenty of medicine for colds, coughs and croup, but he had something different and we were afraid we might give him the wrong thing. He was sick for about a week, and I decided then a cowranch one hundred miles from a settlement might be all right for an old bachelor, but is no place for women and children.

But we got through the winter pretty well, and when spring opened up and grass got good, we had lots of sport with the dogs. We went over towards Grand River, and one of us would go down in the brakes with the trail hounds, the other staying on the divide with the halfblood and greyhounds, and when the dogs got to making it too hot for Mr. Wolf, he would pull out on the divide, then the greyhounds would pick him up, and the wolves got scarcer all the time.

Just before we turned the cattle out of the pasture that spring I got my first white-tailed deer. I went down in the pasture to look after some cows and calves and left my horse standing close to the foot of the mountain, then went up about fifty yards against the mountain to a spring to get a drink of water. When I started back to my horse not fifty feet from my horse stood a big white-tail buck. My rifle was on the saddle, so it was either try him with my six-shooter or let him go. So I pulled down on him, and when the gun cracked he started out just like I had missed him, but he only ran about fifty yards before he fell. I had shot him through the lungs. That was the only white tail deer I ever heard of being killed in the Hills.

We had to have some supplies pretty early that spring. So the first of May I decided to go to Dickinson. Alden Hamilton had moved to North Grand River and his wife and two children had been with him that winter, so my wife wanted to visit them. She and the children went that far with me and I planned to stop for them as I came back. It was twenty miles to their ranch, which is about six miles south of where Bowman, N. Dak., now is. I was gone five days, as the roads were quite soft and spongy. I camped out and cooked my meals. Grass was pretty good for my horses. While I was in Dickinson, I hired a hand for the summer and he came back with me. It rained the night we got back to Alden's and we had to lie over a day for the gumbo to dry.

We got home to find Jone pretty busy, as the rain made water everywhere for the cattle, and the grass, being young and tender, caused the cattle to wander farther out and the range cattle to come in on our range. It took lots of riding to keep them in order.

By the time I got through the winter I was certain I did not want to keep the family on the ranch another winter, and more than that, settlers were coming in, taking up the range and beginning to grumble about men fencing up land they did not own. We would find our gates open when I knew it was no accident, so I thought it would be a pretty good idea to get out before we were forced to take down our fence.

After we got things in pretty good shape and had a

couple of hands to run things, the women folks wanted to go down to Belle Fourche to do some trading and visit with the home folks a short time. We went in the spring wagon so we could make the trip in two days and not camp out, as the mosquitoes were getting pretty bad and would be hard on the children. We put up at our usual stopping place, Macy.

Back twenty-five or thirty years ago it was the fashion to keep the children as free from tan as possible—just as much on the extreme against tan as they are now to get it. So our little boy had been taught to wear his hat, or the sun would burn him black. Our children had not yet seen a negro. While we were in a store in Belle Fourche, the children were looking out and saw a negro man go along the street. Our boy ran to his mother in great excitement shouting "Mama, I saw a man on the street and he had been out in the sun a long time without his hat, for he was black as could be."

We let it be known while in town that our horses, cattle and ranch were for sale. After visiting for a few days, we went back north and found the boys talking wolf hunt. They had been hearing them over toward the badlands on the head of Grand River. They had never seen a wolf chase, so in a day or so we all went out for a hunt. As the boys wanted to see the chase, Jone stayed with them on the divide and kept the greyhounds, and I took the trailers down in the brakes to see if we could get a wolf started. It was not long until they struck a trail and after they ran for about an hour, they were making it pretty interesting for the wolf. He thought it best to cross the divide for the brakes on the head of Bull Creek, but as he was crossing, the greyhounds (on the watch all the time) saw him, and the chase was in full swing. There was a three or four mile stretch of smooth country between the rough land on Grand River and that at the head of Bull Creek, so after the wolf left one for the other, there was no shelter for him and the dogs overhauled him before he had gone a mile. As usual, the fun was over before the trailers or I arrived on the scene. The boys thought it great sport.

The June berries were ripe now, and they were certainly plentiful in the canyons just back of our house near the big spring. I am sure a wagon load could have been gathered in a very short time.

A few days after we got back to the ranch, Tom Mc-Cumsey came to see us and told us there were some men in Belle Fourche who wanted to form a company and buy a ranch with a bunch of well bred cattle. They had sent him out to look the ranch and cattle over and get our price. He was there two days and after he had seen the cattle he said they were the kind he wanted. The location suited him for a good cowranch, but he thought $30.00 per head straight was more than the company would want to pay. We told him it took that to buy them, and that that price only stood for ten days.

It was now time to begin haying. Tom went away but was back inside of a week and said he would give the $30.00 if we would throw in the ranch, which we decided to do, provided that he would give the two boys who were working for us jobs. We sold them all our saddle horse, except two, at the same price as the cattle, and were to count the cattle to them at $30.00 they to get the brand and be entitled to any cattle they might gather after the count. We were to stay and look after the cattle until July 15.

We had now sold the ranch and cattle, but had our range horses yet and no sale for them, as one could hardly give a mare away at that time. We offered them for ten dollars per head, and at that agreed to throw in the spring colts. They were a fine bunch of Percheron mares, with a number of two and three year old geldings, but they were too big for saddle horses.

One day Albert Clarkson came down and said he would trade us his cattle for our horses, and we made a deal. We gave him $26.00 per head and he threw in the calves, while we let him have the horses at $10.00, the colts going in with their mothers. We turned over 125 head of horses, and he had about 50 head of cattle.

As Jone was not wanting to leave the Cave Hills, he bought the Table Mountain ranch from Clarkson, and when we gave possession, he moved up there. I sold him my share of the cattle, and we both kept a good team and saddle horse apiece. When McCumsey came out, we gave him the dogs, as I had no further use for them and Jone decided he did not want them. My wife sold her organ to Mrs. Alden Hamilton and I loaded all our household goods that were worth moving in my wagon, Jone took the two families in the spring wagon and we started for the Belle Fourche valley. As Jone could travel much faster than I, he went on to Macy and I camped on the road when night came on. He got to his father-in-law's the second evening and stopped with them over night. This was on Indian Creek, and the worst mosquito country I ever saw. My wife said they almost carried her and the children off that night.

I have spoken about Ed Labree working for us and running the Table Mountain ranch while we owned it, but in passing, I think I should say more about such a man as he.

Before we hired him, I knew nothing about him other than what he told me. He was a French Canadian, born on a ranch. His mother died while he was a small boy, and his father married again. He and his step-mother did not get along well, so when he was twelve years old, he ran away and fell in with some cow-men out in the western part of Canada. He worked for and with the same outfit until he was twenty-five years old, then started to rove, and had been over most of Canada and the U. S. in his travels. He understood the handling of cattle and horses and was the greatest worker I ever saw at all kinds of ranch business. He never drank anything stronger than water, not even coffee, did not gamble, could not read or write, but never forgot anything he was told or heard read, scarcely ever went to town or visiting, but liked company. He never was in town during the two years he worked for us, always sending by us for what he wanted. He never drew any more of his wages than what he actually needed.

When we sold the Table Mountain ranch and he hired to Clarkson, I wanted to pay him what we owed him. He said no, to keep it until fall, as he was going to Alaska before long and would want it then. He worked for Clarkson until fall, then came down to my place on the river, stayed over night with us and told me he was starting to Alaska. He said he would go to the state of Washington and work in a lumber camp until spring, and then go on. I went with him to Belle Fourche and paid him what we owed him. He cashed the check from Clarkson and with what cash he had made in all, had something over $2,500.00. I wanted him to buy a draft with most of it, but he said "No, I want it all in cash, as I cannot write and I know no one up there. I might have trouble getting it cashed."

I went with him to my friend Charlie Small, the clothier, and he bought a new outfit from hat to boots, put them on, went to a photographer and had a half-dozen photos taken, paid for them, and told me when he got located, he would have someone send me his address—for me to keep one and send the others to him. I asked him if he did not want one sent to his father. He said "No, I heard five years ago he was dead, and if it is so, I have no other near kin." I bade him good bye and he left that evening.

Some time that winter I met Charlie Small on the street. He said, "You have a photo of that fellow you brought to the store last fall, haven't you?"

I said, "Yes, six of them."

He said, "I got a letter from a sheriff near Seattle that a man had been murdered near a lumber camp in that county, and his clothes had my address on them."

I sent a photo to the sheriff, and it proved to be Ed.

And so, a mighty good man, although a queer one in some respects, passed to the great beyond by a murderer's hand.

My mother had moved to Minnesela and bought several

vacant lots that were under the ditch, so she could always raise a good garden and all kinds of fruit.

I did not get to Arpan's until the morning of the second day after the others, and they were all ready to move on with me and get out of the mosquitoes. We all went on to mother's.

We thought we would go to central Nebraska and locate near some town where we could have the advantages of good schools. I had been raised a farmer and wanted to go where the seasons were more certain. It had been very dry in the valley for the last three years, and the dry-farmers had not raised much. I fixed my wagon up for travel, as we thought we would go through in the prairie schooner, and when we got a location to suit us, I would have my three horses. We stored our goods and planned to have them shipped when we got settled. They did not amount to much anyway.

The weather was terribly hot and dry, but about Aug. 10, we got started. My wife was not well, and neither were the children in good condition. We started in the afternoon and drove as far as the Jones horse ranch on Big Bottom the first day, and that night both children were sick all night. So we did not move until afternoon next day and then went only as far as Sturgis. That night the wife and children were all sick, so next morning I concluded it would not do to try to travel with the family while it was so hot. We turned back that morning and got to mother's that night. After a few days they all got better and we thought it would be better for Mrs. Hamilton and the children to go back to West Virginia and stay until I found a location, so they took the train for the East.

I began to think it might be just as well after all to stay in S. Dak. and I started to look around for an irrigated farm. I went up in the Spearfish valley and found some for sale, but thought they were all too high in price. Finally I decided I could make a very good living if I owned enough dry land around my farm to handle some good cattle, so I bought mother's homestead, as it had a good house and fairly good sheds and corrals. It and my homestead joined one another and were fenced. I gave mother $1500.00 for her place, then Fred Stearns had 320 acres adjoining me on the north which was also fenced, and bought it for $1500.00. The Government had an isolated forty acres next to my homestead, and I added that for $1.25 per acre, making 680 acres, all in one body, and every foot nice smooth land. I might mention here that in a very few years after I sold this tract, the government began a huge irrigation project in the valley which brought water to almost all the 680 acres.

A school was on one corner of my land, and a good country store and post office just across the river. I did not know just how my wife would feel about me buying dry land, but I wrote her what I had done and she wrote back that if it suited me, it was all right with her.

Mother and I rented our homesteads, and a man was living in the house, but I bought him out and he moved away. He had a pretty good crop of corn on my place and some on mother's, and Stearns had some on his which I got with the land. There was fine grass on all which had never been broken, so I had lots of feed for a good bunch of cattle to winter on.

I moved right in and began to get ready for the family to come home when their visit was out. I cut up all the corn, fixed up my sheds and hauled up wood for the winter. Most of it came from the Black Hills. I could go up and cut, load my wagon that day, camp that night, and get home by noon the next day. I hauled big loads, as the only pull I had was in crossing the river.

Lots of my old neighbors had gotten discouraged and left their farms, for the last three years had been very dry in the valley. Dry ranches had yielded very little.

I decided I wanted a small bunch of good cattle, so I got in touch with a man at Mason City, Iowa, who had

Shorthorn cows for sale. I went down to see them and bought 25 head of cows and heifers. There was a good demand for well-bred bulls, for nearly all of the small cowmen and ranchers saw the advantage of better cattle. I had plenty of feed for the winter and figured I could keep twenty five or thirty cows on the 680 acre ranch. I got the cows home in February. We didn't have a hard winter, and as there had been no cattle on the place for three years, I had to feed very little. The cows all came through the winter in fine shape.

My wife and children came home in the early part of the winter, and my wife's niece, Miss Sadie Showalter, came with them to make her home with us. She had been suffering from asthma for several years and we thought the high dry climate might be of benefit to her. And it was, for she was entirely well in three months after she got to Dakota.

On March 6, 1898, our third child was born, a boy, and we named him Ray Showalter. He was a very large baby and is now a very large man. After the baby was born, my wife was seriously sick for two months. There were two doctors in Belle Fourche, and I had them both but they did not help her any, and no one thought she could live. I called my cousin, Dr. Baker, at Sundance, Wyoming, and he came at once, staying right with her for a week. He said he had been suffering with rheumatism most of the winter and had been trying to keep in out of the weather and rest up, so he thought a few days rest at our home would do him good. He said when he first came that he could not cure her, but that he could help her and give her ease, but it would be a long time before she could be up and walk. I am sure he saved her life by staying with us, and we have never forgotten the great service he rendered us. Our neighbors were also all very kind to us and helped in many ways. Leading among them was our "Aunt Mag" Hamilton. She would often come and stay, and would do everything she could. My mother and sister came, and took the baby back with them and kept him while Mrs. Hamilton was so very ill. I hired a man to do my plowing and putting in the crop and I was at the house all the time to help with the children, and I had a nurse to look after my wife.

But with all the care, she was not able to be up until the middle of the summer, and then she had to walk on crutches for six months. I will never forget how glad we all were when she was able to walk a little and came to the table with the rest of us.

My cows did fine and most of them brought calves that spring, and I had several orders for bull calves before they were ready to wean. I raised a pretty good corn crop, but I cut the wheat, oats and barley for hay, as I needed hay more than grain. I raised ten bull calves that year and sold them for $50.00 per head.

I thought I would try raising a few good hogs and sent to Davenport, Iowa for a Poland-China sow. She raised me ten pigs, and as not many men were raising hogs in that part of Dakota then, there was not much demand for breeding stock, but I sold a few of them for that purpose, and I butchered and sugar cured a good many and got fancy prices for the sugar cured bacon and hams. Jim Craig was foreman for the Three-V then, and I sold him a dozen hams. John Clay, of Clay, Robinson & Co. of Chicago, was a stockholder in the Three-V and was out to the ranch and ate some of the ham. After that he had me ship him a dozen hams every fall after it was cured, and Jim always bought all the bacon I had to sell. So I had no difficulty in disposing of all the hogs I could raise.

In the fall of '98, my brother Jone sold his Table Mountain ranch and cattle to Fred Stearns and came in and bought the Gartley place of 160 acres, and the Vanaken place, also a 160 acre tract, then put up a new house and decided to go to farming. It was a good farm, being mostly bottom land, lying just a mile west of our farm. He now had two little boys, and had decided as we had, that a cow-ranch is no place on which to rear children.

That fall, my friend and neighbor, Charlie Schlosser, went with a carload of horses to New York state. While there disposing of his horses, he took a severe cold and in a few days developed pneumonia, dying within a week. It certainly was a shock to all his friends, for he was such a strong and healthy young man. I had often heard him say he had never been sick a day in his life. He had a brother, John, living over in Wyoming, who came and took charge of his ranch after his death. He soon sold the ranch and moved the horses to Wyoming, and I rented the homestead, as it joined my land on the west. Charlie, being a horse man, did not farm any, and consequently had broken very little prairie on the homestead. It bordered the river and made an ideal summer pasture for my cattle. As so many were leaving their dry ranches, rent was very cheap. I got the use of this place for paying the taxes each year, which amounted to about thirteen dollars, and I kept it as long as I kept my cattle.

In the fall of '98 my friends elected me County Commissioner for the central district. H. J. Widdows was elected in the western district, and Peter Edwards for the eastern. Butte county was financially embarrassed at the time, and we were paid in warrants which were worth about sixty cents on the dollar. I did not sell any of mine, but bought a few at that price, and it was not long until they were at par.

In the spring of '99 I put out about 100 acres of small grain of different kinds and forty acres of corn. My wife was not well by any means, but was so much better than we thought she ever would be, we were very thankful. Sadie got along fine with the children and I do not know what we would have done had it not been for her.

Uncle Will Hamilton bought ten acres in the suburbs of Spearfish, built a house and set out an orchard, preparing to take it easier in his old days. Alden Hamilton's wife died very suddenly in June '99 and left him with three small children. They were still living on the cowranch on Grand River, and he could not keep the children there, so he brought them to his parents in Spearfish.

My herd of Shorthorns were doing nicely. I got a fine

crop of calves in the spring of '99 and our hogs were doing well. I was considered one of the big hog men of that locality, but would not have made much of a showing among the hog raisers of the cornbelt, as I never had more than thirty or forty on hand at a time. But that was lots of hog up there.

Our settlement had thinned out now so we had no Sunday school or church, and talk was being made of moving the schoolhouse across the river, as nearly all the children in the district lived on the south side. We on the north side were very much opposed to such a move, but we could do nothing. They had water on the south side of the river and the settlers were staying with their ranches, while the ones on our side were getting discouraged and leaving. Too many of them had tried to make it by farming alone and did not handle any kind of stock, and those hot dry years just put them out of business. Had it not been for my cattle, I should have been in the same fix.

The summer of '99 was a pretty good season, and we had a good crop of mosquitoes—that was always a sign of a good crop year. I had about forty acres of land on the half section I had bought from Fred Stearns which had been broken, but never cultivated. It had reset to "gramma" or wheat grass, and that made the best hay I ever saw when cut at the proper time. It would fatten cattle and horses without any grain at all. This forty was extra good the summer of '99, and as I had my cattle on the Schlosser place all the fore part of the summer, I did not need it for pasture.

I had gotten a new mowing machine for this harvest, and one morning about the middle of July, I hooked up a pair of bay Percherons that I had not worked for some time and drove over to this forty to begin cutting. I had been mowing for about an hour and everything was going nicely. I was just thinking how well I was getting along for it was an extra good team, and they were stepping right out like they were going some place, when the cutter bar ran over an old prairie dog hill and I think the sickle must have thrown a little gravel which struck the off horse. He jumped, and then the other horse jumped, then they both jumped, and by that time we were really going some place, and going fast, too. When that cutter began to wave up and down in front of me I thought it was time to change position, so I let go and rolled off behind, and that was a pretty race they had—a half mile to run straight north before they came to the fence. The near horse out ran the other just enough to turn to the right, so as to turn the cutter bar away from the fence, then they had another half mile to run before they came to the fence running along the road. That made a mile race on a perfectly level piece of ground. By the time they got to the end of the mile, they were down to a very slow trot, and brother Jone, who happened to be going along the road at that time, stepped in front of them and halted them. He got on the machine and drove back to meet me.

They had broken nothing but the Pitman rod. I drove them to the house, hitched to the spring wagon and drove to Belle Fourche, eight miles away, got a new rod, and was back mowing just afternoon, and that was the last time that team tried to run away with me.

We got a nice lot of good hay, and got it up in good condition. That was one thing of cutting hay up in that country—not much danger of getting it spoiled with rain. My wheat, oats and barley were fairly good, and my corn was fair. We always raised lots of melons and squash. I had a nice bunch of hogs that fall. I had a feed mill and ground wheat and barley, mixed some millfeed with it, and that was the secret of having good bacon. Wheat, barley, and ship, with a little corn, make much better bacon than all corn diet. We could get one hundred pounds of ship or bran for a bushel of wheat. Wheat was selling for about fifty cents for a bushel for the best grade.

I had planted five acres of corn from seed I got from Nebraska, a large yellow variety, and it was just in good roasting ear by the middle of September. On the 23rd, we had a snow lasting all day and part of the night. Next morning there was about two inches of snow on the ground, and that cornfield was the prettiest thing I ever saw—everything white except that big green corn standing out in the middle. I never expect to see anything like it again. The snow went off that day and it did not freeze that night. I cut the corn immediately and it dried before a freeze, making fine cow-feed.

I sold nearly all my bull calves that fall and butchered a good many hogs selling some of them dressed in Deadwood and Lead City, and making bacon out of some of it. I also sold lots of sausage and lard. I remember I killed fourteen one day. It was pretty cold and I did not have but two men to help, and things went slowly. It was late in the afternoon when we got them all dressed and we carried them to the house. I left them to be cut up the next day, and that night it turned much colder. The next day I was all day cutting those hogs up, they were frozen so hard.

After Uncle and Aunt went to Spearfish, we missed them very much. Our neighbor McMaster moved to Belle Fourche, and Sam Wheeler was elected county treasurer, so he moved his family to town. The Vanaken family moved to the Hills, the Sassa family back to Lead City, the Wright family to Minnesela, and lots of the bachelors left their ranches. In fact, the May family, my brother and ourselves were the only families left on the north side of the river in our school district. There was not one child of school age in the district on our side, so they moved the school house across the river, one mile west.

I did not like the looks of things, we didn't think we could ever get water on our side for irrigation, and all who had tried artesian wells had failed to get water north of the river, though plenty could be gotten on the south side within four hundred feet. Almost all of the settlers who had left their claims had borrowed all they could get on them, and that meant the mortgage companies would own them in a short time. It looked as though we would be left alone.

We had a pretty severe winter in '99-'00, with several bad blizzards, but I had plenty of feed and got my cattle through in fairly good condition. The next spring brother Jone said he had all the farming he wanted, sold his place to McMaster, and went back to the Cave Hills, buying the Curliss ranch on the north side of the hills, and bought another herd of cattle.

When a man starts handling stock on the range, something gets in his system which makes him want to stay. I do not know what it is, but it is there, and I do not believe that a man who has followed the cattle business on the open range for any length of time, either as an ordinary cowboy or an owner, ever gets over the desire to go back to the free and outdoor life it affords. I have been away from it now for more than thirty years, but that desire is just as strong as it ever was, although I know I did the proper thing by leaving it when I did, and I am glad we were able to make the change while the children were young. I do not say that children cannot have the advantage of an education when reared in a thinly settled range country, but is much harder to do, and very unpleasant when the children have to be away from their parents, or the family separated during the school term. I know some of my cousins stayed in the stock business and gave their children good educations. But would we all do it, or would be keep them on the ranch and make cowmen of them? The stock business is just as honorable as any other legitimate business, and it takes just as much brains and judgment to make a success of it, but it is much harder to follow, and a much more trying existence than many other occupations in life.

In the spring of 1900, I continued to rent the Schlosser place, and I put out a pretty good crop of small grain. I tried a new kind of grain called spelt, or at least it was new in that part of the state. It was especially good for hogs when ground. I put up a windmill at a well near the house which was quite an improvement. It saved pumping water for house and barn.

I was now thinking of selling out and moving to some

country where the seasons were more certain, and we might at the same time be where we could educate the children. I never had the advantage of an education, and I knew how hard it was without one.

I had lots of buyers for my cattle, but no one seemed to want land. A company had drilled a well something more than nine hundred feet deep north of Belle Fourche, back north of the river a short way, but struck no water, so it looked like we would never get any artesian water on that side of the river.

In August, 1900, Uncle Jim Hamilton came out to visit us. He had never been in Dakota but had been on the plains of Kansas, Nebraska, and as far up as southern Wyoming in 1866, when he had been sent out just after the war. His command had not been disbanded, and they were sent to guard the frontier against the Indians. He said he had always wanted to see the Black Hills, but they were not allowed to go that far into the Indian country at that time.

On Sept. 1, he and I started in a buggy for the Cave Hills to see Jone and our cousins. We planned to go as far as the Fred Ernest ranch the first day. It rained on us about five miles south of the Ernest ranch, and we fought gumbo the rest of the way, getting to Fred's about nine that night. The next morning it still looked like rain, and we did not start on until afternoon, stopping that night with a friend of mine on Clark's Fork, who had settled there after we had sold our cow ranch. The next day we made it to my brother's ranch, and he was certainly surprised, as he had not heard of Uncle being in Dakota, and had not seen him since his visit in W. Va. We had a fine time visiting around with our relatives and my old friends, and were gone two weeks from the time we started.

I hauled my wood and got ready for winter. I had lots of orders for bacon. Mr. Clay of Chicago wanted two dozen hams, and Jim Craig of the Three-V ranch, all the bacon I had to spare, so that I had no difficulty in disposing of my fat hogs. I sold the ribs, back-bones, and sausage in the

towns of the Hills at a good price. Fred Fuller of Belle
Fourche was wanting my cattle, but I had plenty of feed
to carry them through the winter and was in no hurry to
sell them. We had a fine fall, and the winter was mild up
to Christmas, when it set in very cold. On Jan. 1, we had
a pretty bad blizzard and it continued cold all through the
month, but with very little snow. It turned warmer the last
of February, and the ice went out of the river the first
week in March, the ground thawed out, and it began to feel
like spring.

We had definitely decided to sell at some price, so I did
not farm very heavily in the spring of 1901. I put out about
fifty acres of small grain and twenty-five acres of corn. A
man by the name of Jones came down from Bear Lodge Mt.
in Wyoming and bought all the calves I had wintered, giving
me $50.00 per head for them. Fuller was still wanting my
cattle, so in June I priced them to him at $50.00 per head
and he took them. I thought that if I let the grass grow
on the ranch I would stand a better chance to sell. I had
two or three prospects, and I wanted the place to look its
best when they came to inspect it.

After I got my corn laid by, I decided to go up and
see Dr. Baker and family at Sundance. It was about sixty
miles, and I went up in about one day horseback, stayed a
couple of days, and when I was ready to go home, the doctor
said if I would wait until afternoon, he would go as far as
Sand Creek with me, and we could catch some fine trout.
We had an old friend living at the head of Sand Creek we
could put up with for the night. We got there about sundown and Uncle Josh said, "I will put your horses up and
you fellows can go catch a mess of trout for supper."

The head of the creek was a big spring, the water
boiling up making a big pool something more than forty
feet across, and starting a stream about ten feet wide and
a foot deep. I baited my hook and threw it in the spring,
and it had no more than hit the water until a trout had it
and was gone. I pulled him out and he certainly was a

beauty, about ten inches long, and weighing a pound. If I remember correctly, we caught about half a dozen, all about the same size, took them up to the house, dressed them, and Uncle Josh cooked them just right. I think I enjoyed that meal the best of any I ever ate. I have eaten many kinds of fish before and since that time, but none tasted as good as those speckled trout.

We caught some more for breakfast that were just as good, and we fished a while before I started home. I wrapped a half dozen up in my slicker and tied them on behind the saddle and took them home with me for the wife and children.

That was the last long ride I took on my favorite saddle horse. We read in many books about cowboys and cowmen, how much they thought of a certain saddle horse, and about what a large part the horse had in all their adventures. And it is certainly true to life. It makes no difference how many good horses you may have owned and ridden, there is always one which stands at the head of the list. And so Old Fox stood at the head of mine.

To start with, I think he was the prettiest two year old I ever saw, and he was as wild as they can get. My first admiration for him was as a two-year old, while we were branding colts. During the roping in the corral, he jumped the corral fence and only touched it very lightly with his hind feet as he went over. The fence was seven feet high.

I said to Jone, "That is my horse if I can ever break him."

That fall I caught him and broke him to the halter and picket and turned him with the saddle bunch. The spring he was three, I broke him to ride. He did not buck much and was not vicious in any way, but was just wild.

He was a pretty, bright bay, fifteen and a half hands high, and when mature, weighed a little over one thousand pounds. He was not as fast as some horses I have owned but could start quicker and turn on less ground than any horse I ever rode. He had the best wind of any horse with which I ever drove a bunch of horses, and after he got his full weight, could pull more by the saddle horn than any horse I ever saw. I pulled a 1300-pound steer out of a bog once which a pretty good team had failed to move. When I started him after a critter in a herd, he never lost him. When roping, no difference how often I missed, he kept right after the animal until I made the catch, then he stopped and kept the slack out of the rope until I called for slack. I never was afraid to leave him with any kind of animal tied to the horn, for I was sure it would never get him tangled in the rope. I have left him on the prairie for hours, and if I left the reins down, he was always there near, grazing, when I returned. He might buck with me a little sometimes, but my wife could get on him and take all three of the children, and he would never make a misstep.

So why would not anyone get attached to such a horse? My greatest regret in leaving So. Dak. was in parting with my faithful old horse. He was ten years old when I sold out, and I left the state in 1901.

In September, one of my neighbors said his brother-in-law, a miner, wanted to buy a place, and he would like him to take mine if I were going to sell. I told him what price would buy it, he came to look at it, and we made a trade. I had not threshed my grain yet, and I was the only one on my side of the river who had any to thresh. To make the deal, I agreed to sell at five dollars per acre, and throw in the grain in the stack, he to thresh it. So I had our little sale of personal property, and Nov. 1, 1901 we went to West Virginia on a visit and to look for a location.

While in West Virginia, I got in correspondence with W. E. Jameson of Fulton, Missouri, and went there to look the situation over. Fulton was a nice clean town of about four thousand population, had three good colleges, a good high school, and two state institutions, and was surrounded by a good farming country. It appeared to be a healthful place, land was cheap, and above all, I found a very hospitable and sociable people, mostly originally from Virginia and Kentucky, so that I felt at home among them.

So I bought 212 acres near Fulton, and although we have sold and bought a few times, we have never gotten out of reach of Fulton and its schools and churches.

In December 1903, our fourth child was born, a boy, and we named him Harold Henry.

We have all had good health since coming to Missouri, and I have managed to keep the wolf from the door by handling Shorthorn cattle and Poland-China hogs.

The boys all graduated from Westminster College, and the girl from Synodical College. We furnished them a place to live and helped what little we could until they were all through college, but they all did their part, and when not helping on the farm, were doing something to help them get the education they so much desired. And I am glad we moved to a place where it was possible for the children to fit themselves for useful lives, both to themselves and the community in which they live.

I have not said much about the blue sky, how brightly the sun, moon, and stars did shine, nor how sweetly the birds sang in the sparkling dew of the morning; but I have given the story of life on the frontier of Dakota of a young couple reared in the mountains of West Virginia.

Index